◄ THE ONLINE EPICURE ►

THE ONLINE EPICURE

Finding out Everything You Want to Know About Good Cooking and Eating on the Internet

Neil J. Salkind

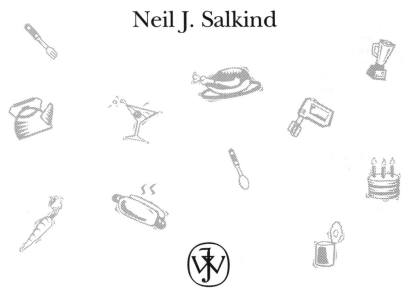

JOHN WILEY & SONS, INC.

New York • Chichester • Weinheim • Toronto • Singapore • Brisbane

Library of Congress Cataloging-in-Publication Data
Salkind, Neil J.
    The online epicure: finding out everything you want to know about
good cooking and eating on the Internet / Neil J. Salkind.
        p.   cm.
    Includes index.
    ISBN 0-471-18019-X (pbk. : alk. paper)
    1. Food—Computer network resources—Directories. 2. Internet
(Computer network)—Directories.   I. Title.
TX357.S244   1997
025.06'641—dc21   96-37792

To my neighbors in Old West Lawrence who know no limits when it comes to good cooking and eating; to Leni (who hums when she eats), who gave me the title for this book and who is my inspiration;

and especially in memory of dear Mike,
who used to eat 12 tacos, 12 doughnuts, and a 6-pack.
We all miss him.

CONTENTS

PREFACE

Those of you who are curious enough to be reading this will not be surprised that this book represents the coming together of two special interests of mine: cooking and computers.

I must credit my interest in cooking, and especially in baking, to my mother, Irene Helen Salkind. My childhood memories are filled with plates of chocolate chip cookies, cream puffs, or rugeluch, cinnamon rolled cookies filled with raisins and nuts, waiting for me on the kitchen table when I returned home each afternoon from school. I used to think I was well liked, until I figured out it was the after-school treats that drew more than one classmate home with me. So the story goes, my maternal grandfather owned a bakery in Brooklyn, and I imagine my mother got at least some of her feel for a pinch of this and a handful of that (no written recipes allowed, please) from her experiences as a child.

I can easily remember watching my mother bake, asking if I could help, and being assigned jobs such as greasing and flouring cake pans, chopping nuts, and even sprinkling the powdered sugar on light, delicate, and delicious cream puffs. I learned that baking and providing good things to eat to those around you is an act of giving that few others can match in generosity, creativity, and satisfaction. My children, good basic cooks themselves, continue in that tradition.

My interest in computers took off in graduate school, when I began computer programming to fulfill a requirement. Within a few years I got hooked on the personal computer as a tool to do my writing. Several books on computers later, a stronger than ever interest in cooking, and the increasingly accessible and interesting Internet (and other online services), made me think that there must be a ton of information about cooking and food online. I was right. It seemed as good as Astaire and Rogers, Laurel and Hardy, and peanut butter and chocolate.

The Online Epicure offers you a guide to online information about cooking, food, and related resources. It covers the major online services, including America Online, CompuServe, and the Microsoft Network, and also provides an extensive review of resources on the Internet, all organized by food category.

The Online Epicure was written with several audiences in mind. Amateur or professional cooks who want to get started using online services and have no experience should begin with "Getting Started Online." Here, you'll find everything from a short history of the Internet to how to use e-mail and surf the Web. Read the second chapter for an introduction to using online services and the Internet for food and cooking information.

Cooks who are already accomplished online computer users can use this book in two ways. First, the table of contents lists 16 different food topics. Go to any of these sections and you'll learn about that topic and what's available online.

Second, the appendix lists all the URLs (or uniform resource locators) mentioned in this book. A URL is the address for a home page on the Word Wide Web. If you need to know more about what a URL is, see "Getting Started Online." There are more than 400 URLs in *The Online Epicure*, and they are all current as of this writing. To avoid having to retype these URLs, go to *The Online Epicure* home page (www.onlineepicure.com) and click on **favorite** for a listing of the home pages. Then just click on the name of the home page and you're on your way.

I hope you have as much fun with *The Online Epicure* as I did writing it. I'm always available via e-mail, so be sure to send me your praises and criticisms, ideas for future editions, and most of all—new home pages to add. Thanks and good eating.

NEIL J. SALKIND
P.O. Box 1465
Lawrence, KS 66044
70404.365@compuserve.com

ACKNOWLEDGMENTS

I have several people to thank, without whom this book would never have been realized. Claire Thompson, Senior Editor at Wiley, gave me the opportunity to undertake the project and offered sound advice and support throughout. Traci Bunkers applied her usually creative talents and made these pages into a book. David Rogelberg, my agent, and his staff at StudioB literary agency typify what agents should be, but often are not: knowledgeable, supportive, enthusiastic, and interested in their authors. I'm especially happy that David, Sherry, and Brian represent me. Finally, to all the cooks at lousy restaurants without whom I would never know what really good food is.

GETTING STARTED ONLINE

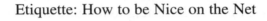

Last night I sat down at my computer and first, found a recipe for salad niçoise. Then I searched for a cooking school I could go to during my August vacation, asked if anyone could help me generate a list of nice Chardonnays under $15 a bottle, and looked for a review of a seafood restaurant in Seattle where business takes me next week. I was going to look for a job in the food industry, but it was too late in the day.

How did I do all this? Using the Internet and some online services such as CompuServe, America Online, and the Microsoft Network. How hard was it to do? Not at all. How much fun was it? Tons. If you stick around, I'll show you how to find out such information and have just as much fun.

You're probably an established cook, be it an amateur or professional, and you're reading this because you want to know what the world of online information can bring to your passion for food and related topics. *The Online Epicure* is your guide to fun and informative food-related sites located online. You don't have to be a rocket scientist to use this book or use the Internet or any online service. In fact, connecting to the Internet or any of the online services is easy, and with their increasing popularity, the price is dropping all the time. So grab your spatula and potholder, turn the stockpot down to a simmer, and read on. If you are already an online star and are familiar with what the Internet or an online service has to offer, you can probably skip this chapter of *The Online Epicure* and move on to whatever chapters of the book focus on your interests.

IN THE BEGINNING, IT WAS THE INTERNET

To understand how you can get information to your computer at home or work by going online, you need to first understand what the Internet is and how it works. In the most basic terms, the Internet is a network of networks. What's a network? A collection of computers connected to one another. For example, America Online is a network of computers, as is CompuServe. My e-mail (electronic mail) address on CompuServe represents a connection to a computer that is one of many connections on that network. If you have an e-mail address on CompuServe as well, then we can e-mail to one another with no need to go outside the network. However, if you have an e-mail address on another network such as America Online, then we can talk with one another only if these two networks are connected. What's the connection? You guessed it—the Internet.

America Online, CompuServe, and the Microsoft Network are all networks that have millions of customers (and computers) connected to one another. Each of those members can communicate with one another through the service. They can also communicate to other people and computers on different services because they have a common connection to the Internet, that huge network that links all the others together. For example, I can e-mail my friend Roz in New York on America Online through my CompuServe account or I can e-mail my friend David in Indiana on CompuServe through my Internet connection.

There are thousands of networks, many of them hosting computers that contain information about everything from recipes for hot sauce to reviews of very fancy restaurants in France. In *The Online Epicure*, I'll show you how to get to these computers and use and enjoy that information.

A (VERY) SHORT HISTORY LESSON

You don't need the following history to prepare a delicious, rich macaroni and cheese dish on a cold winter's night, but it will give you some idea about the origins of the Internet and how to make best use of what it and online services have to offer.

Almost 30 years ago, the Department of Defense thought it a good idea to develop a safe (from nuclear attack) way to connect essential military and government offices and personnel. So was born the grandparent of the Internet, named ARPANET (Advanced Research Projects Agency NET).

From that effort, came other networks such as MILNET (Military NET), BITNET (Because It's Time NET), and NSFNET (National Science Foundation NET). The large amount of exchange over these networks became unmanageable, and a group of people got together to formalize the rules and regulations by which these transfers take place. Eventually the term *Internet* was applied to all of these networks and is now governed by an appointed group of people from the Internet Society. These people make the rules and set the policies for everything from how Internet sites should be named (so that no two are the same) to what's appropriate online behavior.

Although the Internet was born 30 years ago, only during the last 5 years has it become such a popular tool for sharing information electronically. Online activities that were formerly the province of just the Internet have become commercialized by such companies as America Online, CompuServe, the Microsoft Network, and many other online services. These services have been successful because they have made e-mail and other features easy and intuitive to use. For example, to get a recipe from another computer site, early Internet commands would look like a cryptic set of character commands such as `c>ftp get icecream.txt`. Now, using a Windows interface, all it takes is a few clicks of the mouse.

Today, you can connect to the Internet directly through an Internet provider whose only business is connecting people to the Internet or through an online service such as America Online, whose business is providing other online services in addition to connections to the Internet.

WHAT YOU CAN DO ONLINE

If you're talking about activities related to information, there's not much that you can't do online. Here's a brief overview of how the Internet and online services are used.

- Going online is probably used most often for electronic mail, or e-mail. Just as you can exchange mail with a friend or business associate across the United States or the world, so you can do the same without ever placing pen to paper. You create a message and send it to your destination's electronic address. It's fast, easy, and fun.

   For example, you might want to contact the good people at the New England Cheese and Supply (at `http://www.cheesemaking.com/`) and ask them if they have a certain type of cheese culture available.

- Then there's the most popular of all the online features, browsing and using the World Wide Web. The World Wide Web (or WWW or Web) is a collection of home pages, or locations, each of which has a specific address and contains information about a particular topic as well as connections to other home pages on the WWW. An additional bonus is that these graphical home pages are often very nicely designed and organized and fun to use. The majority of what you read about in *The Online Epicure* concerns the location and contents of home pages on the World Wide Web.

For example, an excellent starting point is the Epicurious Food home page (`http://www.epicurious.com/a_home/a00_home/ home.html`) shown on the next page. You can find offerings about eating and drinking, articles from magazines such as *Gourmet* and *Bon Appetit* and much more, including connections to hundreds of other food-related places. All it takes is a click of a button to go to a new location. Once you start roaming around the Web, be ready to spend a considerable amount of time. There is so much stuff and it is all so interesting that you'll find yourself extending those few minutes to a few hours.

- Almost 6,000 electronic newsgroups are available on the Internet. These are places where information can be posted and shared among users—like a conversation place. For example, if your passion is chocolate (and whose isn't?) you can go to `rec.food.chocolate` and get in on the conversation. You can do the same with `alt.restaurants` (to find reviews) and even `alt.fast.food` to find out all you ever wanted (and probably didn't want to know) about Hardee's latest special.
- Information, information, information—all available in millions of files on the Internet. Using file transfer protocol (ftp), you can download or transfer files from other locations to your computer. With a little practice, you can surf the Net for recipes and other cooking-related information.

  For example, recently I turned to the Internet to find an easy recipe for spaghetti carbonara, downloaded it, and had the dish on the table (much to my family's approval) in 30 minutes.
- When you telnet or connect to a remote site, it's as if you were using a computer at another location. With a telnet connection, you can control a computer from thousands of miles away and get the information that those computers have access to. It's like remote control.

  For example, if you're interested in what the holdings are at the Library of Congress on foods prepared and eaten during Colonial times, telnet to the Library of Congress and search the collection.

Eating | Drinking | Playing | Bon Appétit | Gourmet | Home |
Text-Only Index
Go to Epicurious Travel

epicurious
FOOD
OCTOBER 15, 1996

FOR PEOPLE WHO EAT

OKTOBERFEST

Sure, some still
go to Munich, but
why not let the
party come to
you? Click here
for a crib sheet on
beers, celebrations
across the States,
recipes with that
extra oompah-pah,
and more.

Eating

Drinking

Playing With
Your Food

THE FOOD POLL
Stout
or
Lager?

THE WORD OF THE DAY IS **GRASSHOPPER**, AND IT'S IN **THE DICTIONARY**

Menu

The Diva of Endive
Ruth Van Waerebeek makes
the simple superb in her Everybody
Eats Well in Belgium Cookbook

DATES ARE FRESH IN **LOS ANGELES**.
SO **WHAT'S RIPE** IN YOUR FARMERS' MARKET?

Gourmet
MAIN PAGE
THE GOURMET INDEX

BON APPÉTIT
MAIN PAGE
THE BON APPETIT INDEX

HOLY BASIL! HOW TO TELL THE **BASILS** APART, GROW THEM, AND
COOK WITH THEM.

Can We Talk?
So, you've always disagreed with our critic about the essential
restaurants in New York? Here's your chance to speak and be
heard. Or maybe it's just that you want to chat out loud?

RECIPES   **FORUMS**   **SEARCH**   **HELP**

Eating | Drinking | Playing | Bon Appétit | Gourmet | Home |
Text-Only Index
Go to Epicurious Travel

ILLUSTRATION BY ALISON SEIFFER

GODIVA
GODIVA
Holidays

THE 10 ONLINE COMMANDMENTS

These didn't come down from a mountain nor are they inscribed on stone tablets, but they're good advice.

COMMANDMENT #1. YOU'RE A BEGINNER, BE REASONABLE.

You're a cook, not a computer scientist. Even though the material in *The Online Epicure* is not difficult to master, you need to take your time and work carefully. Should you make a mistake, join the club; you will surely not launch any intercontinental ballistic missiles nor cause a stock market crash as a result of the error. So, give yourself the luxury of exploring (perhaps the most fun!) and making errors. How else can you learn?

COMMANDMENT #2. ONCE YOU PRESS THE KEY, IT'S OVER.

There's no recalling keystrokes. Once you press that enter key or execute a command it's done. This is especially important when it comes to e-mail. Once you send that angry letter, there's no going to the mailbox and fishing it out. You need to be extra careful and extra sure of what you say and what you want to do, before you do it electronically.

COMMANDMENT #3. TYPING COUNTS, AND SOMETIMES CASE DOES AS WELL.

One of the idiosyncracies of online services (and especially the Internet) is that uppercase letters (such as A, B, C) and lowercase letters (such as a, b, c) are interpreted differently. Many Internet connections require you to use uppercase characters to sign on. If your password is SARA, then sara may not work. Also, typing accurately really counts. The Internet often demands long names and addresses. It's easy to type *njs@falcon.cc.ukans.eud*, rather than *njs@falcon.cc.ukans.edu*, and spend the next hour trying to figure out why mail was never delivered. New Internet users (often called *newbies*) spend time trying to figure out why their Internet connection doesn't work when the problem is that they incorrectly typed an address.

COMMANDMENT #4. BE FLEXIBLE ABOUT WHEN AND HOW YOU USE AN ONLINE SERVICE OR THE INTERNET.

Online connections can be very busy places, especially during business hours. If you choose to work during these hours, you'll need to be patient because it will take longer to do almost everything. Better yet, work on your online activities after dinner, during the late evening hours, or even on the weekend. Traffic is usually less congested because institutional, research, and business users are not online at these times.

COMMANDMENT #5. DO YOUR OWN STUFF.

Online services and the Internet are what they are—repositories of information, but not substitutes for creativity or hard work. For those, you'll have to look to yourself.

COMMANDMENT #6. THERE'S MORE STUFF OUT THERE THAN ANYONE CAN KNOW ABOUT.

When you go online for the first time you probably won't be able to contain your enthusiasm for what's ahead of you. That's great, but don't get carried away. There are millions of resources available for you to access and use. It will take you months to find everything, and even then, there will be more because the amount of online information is increasing so rapidly.

COMMANDMENT #7. BE CONSIDERATE OF OTHERS AND PLAY BY THE RULES.

No one central authority controls every computer network on the Internet. Even online services have rules, but they are rather general. A set of informal and unenforced rules of etiquette have evolved however. Most users follow these unwritten rules, because if they didn't all online activity would be chaotic and unproductive. We'll give you the basics on etiquette shortly.

COMMANDMENT #8. PRACTICE, PRACTICE, PRACTICE.

The more you practice, the more you will learn and the more rewarding your online activities will be. When you first get started, however, take your time and limit your efforts to an hour or less. This will prevent you from becoming fatigued and frustrated. The more you practice, the more cool and useful locations you'll find.

COMMANDMENT #9. BE PATIENT WITH YOURSELF.

Learning to go online is not like learning to use a new word processor or play a new game. There is little documentation and no one program to run everything. If you have difficulty at first, don't quit. Follow the examples in this book, read as much as you can about the Internet, attend classes if they are offered in your area, and talk to others. Above all, explore and don't take anything too seriously.

COMMANDMENT #10. ASK OTHERS FOR HELP, AND HELP OTHERS.

A tremendous amount of valuable information comes from other users rather than from books (except this one, of course!), user manuals, write-ups, and technical papers. Find out who in your neighborhood or at work might have some insight into using the Internet and online services. If you subscribe to an online service, be sure to use online help. Finally, ask politely for help from others and pay back that debt by helping others when you learn new and interesting things.

ETIQUETTE: HOW TO BE NICE ON THE NET

Commandment #7 stressed the importance of being considerate of others and playing "by the rules." Where do these rules come from, and what are they? For the most part, these rules have evolved out of the need for some order on the Internet. They have been suggested by everyday online users like you and me.

They don't unreasonably restrict anyone's behavior, but they make it easier for everyone to carry on their online activities. What follows are some of the general etiquette rules of the Internet. It's up to users (like you and me) to adhere to this communal set of rules.

- Above all, behavior online is the responsibility of the individual. You own your own words, so say what you mean and mean what you say. This is especially true with e-mail and newsgroup contributions.
- Individual differences are to be fostered and respected. You might disagree with someone's opinion about a restaurant review, their view of a raging philosophical debate, or a political viewpoint, but the free exchange of information, not the censorship of that information, is one of the primary goals of online services.
- Don't intimidate, insult, or verbally abuse anyone else. The same good manners you use in your home and everyday interactions with your friends should be used online as well.
- What's yours is yours and what's not is not. Be sure that you don't unintentionally appropriate other people's materials as your own.
- Avoid sending junk mail. You can send the same message about your restaurant to 3,000 people all at once, but junk mail ties up valuable resources and is not an appropriate use of online services.

IF YOU'RE NOT ALREADY CONNECTED, READ THIS

You need four things to get started and go online. The first is a computer. In any telecommunications activity the computer acts as a sender and receiver of information. Most new computers come with the software for America Online and CompuServe already installed. The Windows 95 operating system comes with the Microsoft Network already installed and ready for you to use with a click on the MSN icon.

Second, you'll need a modem, a standard offering with most new systems. A modem is a device that *mo*dulates and *demo*dulates electronic signals so that they can be transmitted over a telephone line. The modem is located between your computer and the telephone line, and it sits there (and another modem sits on the other end of the phone line) and acts as the grand translator. The faster the modem the better, especially if you want to transfer large amounts of information from one location to another. For example, if you find some clip art to use in a menu you are designing, it will take a considerable amount of time to transfer that art to your own computer if you have a slow modem.

Third, to make all this work, you need communications software. This is the software that translates the information so that it appears to you in the form it was actually sent. Most modems come with some communications software, and most online services provide it as well. Services such as America Online send out hundreds of thousands of free disks each month containing their sign-up software and often sell modems at a reduced price if you subscribe.

Finally, you need a free telephone line to make your connection. If you have only one line for both voice and data, then you cannot talk on the telephone when you are transmitting. Most people who become really serious about online activities install a separate phone line.

CONNECTING TO ONLINE SERVICES

The three biggest online service providers are America Online, the CompuServe Information Service, and the Microsoft Network, with a combined membership of almost 20,000,000. These online services provide you with lots of options. We'll show you what each features in the area of food later in *The Online Epicure*. For now, if you are looking for an online service, you should know that these three have the following in common.

- They all provide quick and easy access to the Internet.
- They all cost about $10 per month for the most basic services, which include e-mail and access to the Internet.
- Their software is relatively easy to use.
- They all offer some free hours, so you can try them out, but you have to sign up first.
- They all offer technical support, although the quality varies considerably.

Here's what I love (and don't love) about each.

America Online (1-800-827-6364) offers its first 10 hours free. After that, several membership options are available. What America Online offers is the largest and most diverse selection of popular sites and a jazzy and attractive interface. It's where you can catch the latest restaurant reviews, visit MTV, find out about new wine offerings, and if the Yankees won last night. What America Online lacks is easily accessible human technical support. For the experienced online user, that may not be a problem. For a beginner, it may be.

CompuServe Information Service (1-800-848-8990) also offers a great introductory deal. The first 10 hours are free, then you have a couple of membership plans to choose from. The basic plan gives you 5 hours per month for your monthly fee, and then it's extra for each hour after that. All plans give you unlimited e-mail use and access to forums (also known as discussion groups). CompuServe Information Service is best known for its extensive collection of forums (with titles such as Cooks Online) and the more than 900 databases that are available. CompuServe also offers very good customer support, and they are the only service to offer an informative magazine published monthly.

The Microsoft Network (1-800-386-5550) also has a terrific introductory offer. It allows you a free 30-day trial, after which you can select from several different plans. The basic plan is 3 hours per month for a small monthly fee, and then you are charged for each additional hour. The good thing about the Microsoft Network is that the Microsoft Corporation is behind it. They want to be #1, especially when it comes to the Internet, so they also are investing lots of resources and offer the latest Internet software. The one shortcoming is that the Microsoft Network is relatively slow, but that is less true today than it was when they first opened. The Microsoft Network also offers excellent customer support.

You can't go wrong with any of these services, and if you don't have any reason to subscribe to one or the other, try each one for a week and see which one is easiest to use and best for you. Keep in mind that if you want to resign from any of these services, you have to call them. Ironically, you cannot resign online.

CONNECTING TO THE INTERNET

You can access the Internet through any one of the three major online services. Once you become a member, you just click on the Internet icon and you're there—pretty easy. You can also establish an account with an Internet provider. You will be able to use the Internet, and such a connection has some of the following advantages as well.

You pay for what you need and nothing extra. With an online service, you pay for the maintenance and services you might not need. With an Internet provider, all you pay for is the connection to the Internet. If all you want is e-mail and Internet access, there's no reason to fool with an online service. Stay with an Internet provider. There's probably one in your own area, so the phone call to connect is not long distance. You can find a list of over 4,000 Internet providers organized by state at `http://thelist.iworld.com/`. Later we'll show you how to visit that Internet site.

ONLINE TIP: KEEPING COSTS DOWN

Lew was visiting America Online to find Chicago restaurant reviews as he planned his trip. What he didn't realize was that the phone connection time was separate from his regular AOL monthly fee. He ended up spending more than $60 just on long-distance charges, even though the city to which he connected was only 20 miles away. The moral is to be careful and check with your online company or Internet provider about special phone lines or local numbers so that you don't incur these charges. Also, be sure to check with your phone company about the per-minute charges for connecting to the service.

- Internet providers are often cheaper because they concentrate on only one service and once you're connected, it's unlikely you'll need the constant attention to maintaining customers that adds cost to the online services. For example, some Internet providers allow for unlimited connection time for $20 or so per month. If you access the Internet through an online service such as the Microsoft Network and spend 20 hours a month (not an unreasonable amount) you will probably end up spending more.

- Internet providers are not as big as online services, and they are probably willing to work harder to get and keep your business. What this means is that they are also willing to provide better support, cheaper prices, good service, and often more flexibility.

USING THE INTERNET

What follows is an introduction to using the Internet. It presents the basics, but it's as much as you need to know to get started. This is a book about cooking and not a computer book, so I don't go into any great depth about how to use the various features of the Internet. You'll find step-by-step instructions to master only the basics.

The applications we use for demonstration purposes to illustrate certain Internet skills are Eudora for e-mail and Netscape Navigator as a World Wide Web browser, the Internet tool that allows you to easily move from one Internet site or home page to another.

Eudora from Qualcomm (800-338-3672) is the most popular e-mail program using a Windows interface. Netscape Navigator by Netscape (415-937-2555) is the most popular Internet browser, but is being hard pressed by Microsoft's Internet Explorer. Using Netscape (or any other browser), you can "surf the net" and go from the Gina Rose Long Life Cooking School to a review of the Atomic Cafe in Lexington, Kentucky, and check out the menu.

We have selected Eudora and Netscape to show you how the Internet works because they are easy to use and inexpensive to purchase (even free in some cases), and they have great technical support. Many other e-mail applications and Web browsers are available as well, and you can easily apply what you learn here to using those tools.

USING E-MAIL: HELLO, MIKE? HOW MUCH BUTTER AND BLUE CHEESE SHOULD I USE?

Here's a real story. I met Mike at the grocery yesterday evening and we talked about his plan to make pesto for that evening's dinner. He also told me about a simple and delicious pasta dish where you mix a blue cheese (such as Gorgonzola) and butter, but he didn't tell me what quantity of each. I didn't plan on making that dish until mid-week, so I e-mailed him for the information.

RECIPE: BLUE CHEESE AND PASTA

This is a rich and delicious dish that serves as a wonderful first course or an entire meal. Serve with a crusty bread and a dry white wine. It's also famed tenor Luciano Pavarotti's favorite pasta dish.

What you need:
Equal parts of a strong blue cheese such as Stilton or Gorgonzola and butter
Fresh parsley

How to make it:
Place the cheese and butter into a sauce pan and heat until they are melted and stir to combine. If you use a microwave, heat for 60 seconds at full power, then stir. Repeat heating if necessary for 30 seconds. Be careful of overcooking. Mix with hot pasta and serve immediately topped with parsley and fresh ground or grated Parmesan cheese.

HOW TO SEND E-MAIL

As with any e-mail application such as Eudora, you start it by double-clicking on the icon. When you see the opening screen, click on **Message**, then click on **New**. Then you'll be ready to compose and send your message as I did in the screen shown on the next page.

Here's how I created the message and sent the mail. Use the Tab key to move from field to field.

1. In the **To:** field, I typed MikeV@grapevine.com. This is Mike's unique e-mail address on Grapevine (an e-mail and Internet service provider). No one else has this address. MikeV is his e-mail name, grapevine.com indicates that he is on Grapevine.
2. In the **From:** field, I typed my e-mail address.
3. In the **Subject:** field, I typed "How Much?" When Mike gets his mail, he will see a list of waiting messages and will be able to tell what the content of any one message is by what was typed in the subject line.
4. In the message body, I typed the contents of the message.
5. I clicked on **Send** Send and the message was sent to Mike.

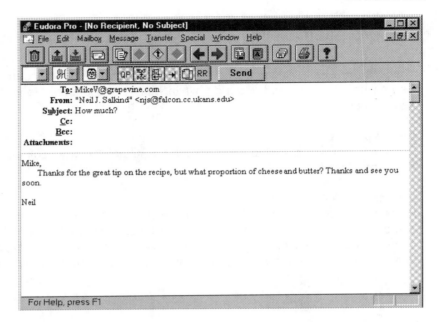

How long will it take to get there? Anywhere from a few seconds to a few hours depending upon the amount of traffic on the various networks that have to connect and talk with one another. When Mike signs on to his Grapevine account the next time, he'll see that he has mail and can then read it and respond.

HOW TO REPLY TO E-MAIL

Replying to e-mail is as easy as sending it. When you open your e-mail application, such as Eudora, you'll see a list of messages that are waiting for you. Just double-click on the message you want to read. First you read the mail, then you reply to it.

To read and reply to my mail, Mike did the following:
1. He clicked on the **Reply** icon
2. In the **Reply** window shown on the next page, he entered the message to me.
3. He **clicked** on the **Send** icon.

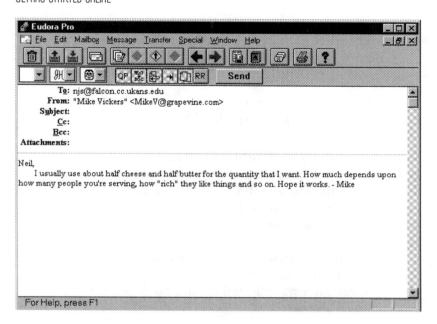

It's as easy as that, and the mail is on its way. This is just about the way that any mailing program works. You create mail and send it, and when you get mail, you reply to it. The biggest challenge is making sure that the e-mail address of the person you want to mail to is correct and that you enter it correctly.

SOME E-MAIL ETIQUETTE

No one's perfect. Here are some hints to help you avoid embarrassing and time-wasting errors during your e-mail activities.

1. Although you think that your mail is private, it may not be. The worst case here is when you reply to a message sent out simultaneously to hundreds of people. Then, everyone on the list sees your reply!

2. Only send those things that you would allow everyone in your organization to see.

3. Once you have finished reading a message, delete it so as to keep active files to a minimum and free up space for everyone. If you want to keep a mail message, save it to your own hard drive.

4. Check your mail on a regular basis. It will help you keep current. Keep your correspondents in mind, and clear unwanted messages when you are done.

EXPLORING THE WORD WIDE WEB

You've heard about the World Wide Web (also known as the WWW or the Web), but what does it do in our quest to find information about food online? The Web is a collection of home pages on the Internet. In order to see and use these home pages (containing links to other home pages), you need a browser such as Netscape Navigator.

There are other viewers such as the Internet Explorer (from Microsoft) and Mosaic (from Spry), and they all work fine. Netscape Navigator was selected for this book because it is the most popular browser.

SAY HELLO TO NETSCAPE NAVIGATOR

You start Netscape as you do any Windows application by double-clicking on the icon that represents the application. When you do this, you'll see the Netscape opening window shown on the next page. In this example, we're already at the home page for *The Online Epicure*, which contains some graphics and text as well as links to other locations or home pages on the WWW.

A BIT ABOUT HOME PAGES

A home page is a collection of information. The home pages you see in *The Online Epicure* have to do with food and drink and related areas, but there are thousands of home pages on the Web dealing with every topic imaginable.

An important element of any home page is the URL or uniform resource locator shown in the **Location:** box at the top of the Netscape window. Just as you use the street address to find a house, so the URL allows any home page to be found on the

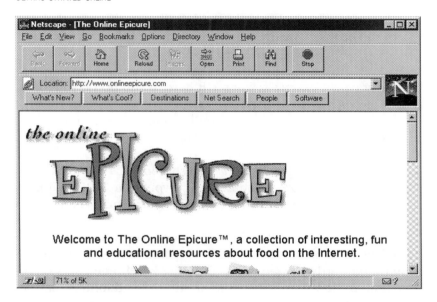

Internet. Once you know the URL for a particular home page, you can just enter it in the **Location:** box, press **Enter**, and Netscape will take you there. For example, you saw the home page for Epicurious Food (`http://www.epicurious.com/a_home/a00_home/home.html`). If you type those URL characters (exactly!) and press **Return**, your browser should take you to that Web site.

All the URLs mentioned in this book are listed in the appendix. They are also available on *The Online Epicure* home page at `www.onlineepicure.com`. All you need to do is click on any of the URLs and your browser will deliver you to the new location.

The Epicurious Food home page includes some text, some icons, and some highlighted words that are links to other pages (such as the link to *Bon Appétit*). When you place the mouse pointer on one of these highlighted words, the pointer changes to a hand shape, and when you click on such a link, you're taken to wherever that link has been programmed to lead.

LOCATING ANOTHER HOME PAGE

If you're not already there, let's visit *The Online Epicure*. Follow these steps:

1. Place the insertion point in the Location: text box at the top of the browser you are using and type the following URL:

   `http://www.onlineepicure.com`

You must type it exactly as you see it here. If you don't, you'll get a message such as *Unable to locate host!*

You may just be able to type "onlineepicure" and your browser will know to add www (for World Wide Web) and .com (for commercial) to the address.

2. Press **Enter**. In a few seconds, you should see *The Online Epicure* home page. If you don't, try typing the URL again. That's all there is to going to a new home page by entering a new URL.

Another way to get to a different home page is by clicking on any of the links on a home page. Try clicking on some of the underlined words you see in *The Online Epicure* home page to go to a different location. Some links are underlined; others may be icons or pictures. The way you can tell if an icon or image is a link is to look at the shape of the mouse pointer when you place it on the suspected link. If it changes to a hand like this 🖑, it's a link. To return to an earlier page, click the **Back** button on the top of the browser you are using.

USING A BOOKMARK

The Web contains so much information about so many things that you'll want to collect your favorite places so that you can visit them later. You can do this quite easily using the Bookmarks menu.

A bookmark is used like a bookmark in any book. It keeps your place until you return later. To create a bookmark, follow these steps:

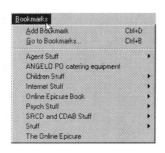

1. Be sure you are in the home page for which you want to create a bookmark.
2. Click on **Bookmarks**, then click **Add Bookmark**.

Once you do this, the title of the home page will be added to your list of bookmarks. Here is an example of bookmarks added to the bookmark menu. All you need to do is click on the bookmark you want to go to and Netscape will deliver you to that home page as soon as possible.

LOCATING HOME PAGES ABOUT FOOD

This is *the* $64,000 question. To begin with, anyone can create a home page, so there's one for the manufacturers of Ragu (http://www.ragu.com/) but there are home pages for three people on my block as well.

There are hundreds of thousands of home pages, but unfortunately, they aren't organized in any systematic fashion. There's no index or card catalog as there is for the books in the library. There's no central listing of home pages, so you cannot go to any one directory or some other source and find something like "All the home pages that deal with cooking chili."

There are two very good ways to find home pages that might contain content for which you are looking. The first way is to explore the Web on your own and talk with your friends and colleagues to find out what they're discovering. When you find a terrific home page, create a bookmark and share that information with a friend.

The second way is to use one of the many search engines that are currently available on the Web. These are specialized search tools that can locate the URLs of Web pages based on the information you provide. Fortunately, the best of these are located in one collection on the All-in-One Search page (http://www.albany.net/allinone/), which lists hundreds of search engines organized in categories such as the World Wide Web, General Interest, and News/Weather.

For example, if I were to click on the Word Wide Web button on the All-in-One Search home page, I would have a choice of over 50 general search engines. I'll select the AltaVista search engine as shown on the next page, then type "chocolate truffles" in the search box and press **Enter**.

The result is 6,000 "hits," where both words occur together, and then a listing of the URLs for home pages that contain the search words I entered. AltaVista makes the judgment that those listed first are those that are closest. The first choice is Kids

---

NETSCAPE TIP: WHERE YOU AND NETSCAPE HAVE BEEN

There's another way to get around from home page to home page besides bookmarks, and that's through the History command on the Window menu. This provides you with a list of places you've been—your history using Netscape, and an easy way to get back to any one of them. To view the history of your Netscape session click on Window, then click on History. You will see a list of the titles of the home pages you have visited as well as the corresponding URL for each one of them. You can then double-click on any page title to go to that page.

Recipes at `http://www.god.co.uk/ynet/text/choc.html`, a home page containing a simple recipe for chocolate truffles.

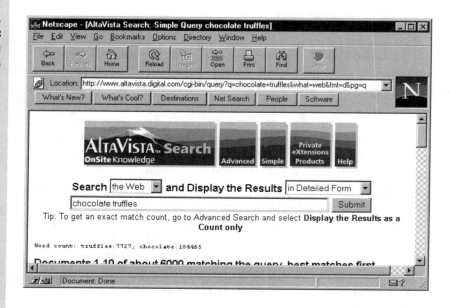

In the People category in the All-in-One Search page, you can use the search engine named EPS or E-Mail Search Program (`http://www.esp.co.uk/`) to find someone's e-mail address or search the AT&T toll-free directory (`http://www.tollfree.att.net/cgi-bin/plsqf_opcode.pl`) to find the toll-free phone number for places like the Williams-Sonoma catalog store.

TEN WONDERFUL WWW SEARCH ENGINES

The All-in-One Search page (`http://www.albany.net/allinone/all1srch.html`) has plenty of search engines that you can click on and use to search for home pages all over the Web. Here is a selection of those that you might find particularly useful, including the name and URL. Remember, if a search engine works for you, create a bookmark!

Here are some tools that search the World Wide Web in a variety of categories.

- Yahoo (http://www.yahoo.com/) is an exciting and innovative search engine that is organized by categories such as science, education, news, health, and recreation. If you use Yahoo, then you're a Yahooligan (click *that* link and see where it takes you)!
- AltaVista (http://www.altavista.digital.com/) is a search engine supported by Digital and claims to be the largest search engine with more than 30 million Web pages indexed.
- Hotbot, supported by HotWired, claims an index of over 54 million Web pages and allows for special search terms using its Expert option.
- Infoseek (http://www.infoseek.com/) is categorized like Yahoo and also offers search tips for beginners and experts, free Web software and InfoSeek QuickSeek, which places a QuickSeek button on the Netscape toolbar, making it very easy to use.

If you want to find someone's e-mail address or if they have a home page, try one of these:

- ESP Mail Program (http://www.esp.co.uk/) requires you to enter a name and then searches for whatever e-mail addresses are associated with that name.
- 411 bills itself as "The best way to search for someone on the Internet." You supply as much information as you have about a person, and 411 will find any e-mail addresses and phone numbers that may be available.

Searching for a publication? Try these:

- Ecola's 24-Hour Newsstand (http://www.ecola.com/news/) allows you to search for more than 2,100 newspapers, magazines, and computer publications that are on the Web, but also appear in print.
- The Electronic Newsstand (http://www.enews.com/) maintains a 2,000 Monster Magazine List containing thousands of articles and allows for a search on keywords.

If you need to search for information in general, try these:

- *Bartlett's Quotations* (http://www.columbia.edu/acis/bartleby/bartlett/) provides a search by word option. That's where I found, "If music be the food of love, play on"—Shakespeare.
- Xerox Map Viewer (http://pubweb.parc.xerox.com/map) provides you with a detailed map of many cities.

DOING AN ADVANCED SEARCH

Most search engines allow for a simple or an advanced search. A simple search looks for the occurrence of whatever words you enter. An advanced search lets you take advantage of logical operators such as AND or OR. So, if I wanted to perform an advanced search to find information on chocolate truffles, I would click on Advanced search options, enter chocolate AND truffles, and then click on Search.

A word of warning! If you're even a little bit of a Web fan, find someone else to raise your children, do your grocery shopping, and do your job, chores, and other obligations. Once you get connected to the Web and start exploring, you'll find it more than easy to spend hour after hour on the Web.

ALL THE NEWS THAT FITS: NEWSGROUPS

Imagine being able to find food-related information on 6,000 topics ranging from chocolate to sushi to ice cream. Where in the world would you be able to find a collection of such diverse information that can be as easily accessed? You guessed it. The Internet and the various sites that ship news each day around the world.

To use a newsgroup, you subscribe to it through your newsreader. You can subscribe to one or 400 newsgroups, and unsubscribe to them as well. When you use a newsgroup, you read the contents and then respond by posting your own contribution. To help manage the flow of newsgroup information, newsgroup sites are managed by system administrators. The newsgroups from which you can select news are those that the system administrator makes available, so you may not have available all the newsgroups you read about here, or hear about from friends.

WHAT'S IN THE NEWS?

Although there are not many restrictions as to what goes on within a newsgroup except for the system administrator's management, newsgroups are named and organized following a set of rules. The most general of these rules has to do with the naming of newsgroups. There are seven major newsgroups, each using a specific label such as rec. for recreation or sci. for science. For example, the rec.food.chocolate newsgroup deals with chocolate under the heading of food, which is under the more general heading of rec., or recreation.

There is also an alternative set of newsgroups, some of which are even more popular than main newsgroups, such as alt. (for anything unusual) and biz. (for business).

WORKING WITH NEWSGROUPS

Working with newsgroups involves

● subscribing and unsubscribing; reading the contents of a newsgroup; and interacting with people in the newsgroup.

SUBSCRIBING TO A NEWSGROUP

When you subscribe to a newsgroup, you are telling the news reader that you want to see all the news about that group. You can subscribe to as many newsgroups as you want, and Netscape will list them all on the Subscribed Newsgroup opening window such as the one here.

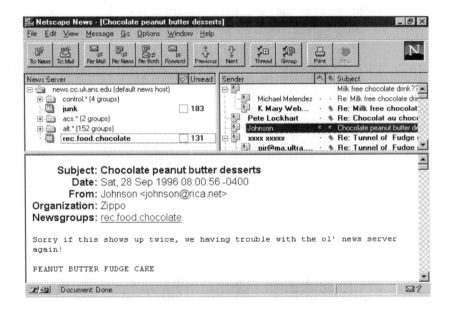

To subscribe to a newsgroup, follow these steps:

1. After you have listed all the newsgroups that are available to you, right-click on the newsgroup you want to subscribe to, then click on **Subscribe**. If you don't see any newsgroups on your screen, you may have to first select the **Show All Newsgroups** option from the **Options** menu.

2. Click on **Options**, then click on **Show Subscribed Newsgroups**. As you see in the previous screen, only those that are subscribed to will appear. Here you can see just a small portion of all those related to food.

If you don't see the newsgroup you want to join among the entire list of newsgroups, then enter it manually. Click on **File**, then click on **Add Newsgroup**, then enter the complete name of the newsgroup (you obviously have to know this), and click on **OK.**

UNSUBSCRIBING TO A NEWSGROUP

Unsubscribing to a newsgroup is just as easy as subscribing. You unsubscribe when a newsgroup is no longer of interest to you or the newsgroup has become defunct and no more news is coming in. Just right-click on the newsgroup name and click on **Unsubscribe**. You just won't see this newsgroup on your list.

READING MATERIAL IN A NEWSGROUP

To see the various articles that are available in any newsgroup, double-click on the name of the newsgroup. In the rec.food.chocolate newsgroup you see a listing of the articles that have already been posted. Double-click on the article you want to read (such as chocolate peanut butter desserts), and the text of that article will appear in the Netscape News Reader screen.

RESPONDING TO NEWS

Now's your chance to reply to a news article.
1. Click on the **Re:News** button at the top of the Netscape screen. When you do this, you are shown a Reply screen where you can enter your response.
2. Enter whatever response you want. Keep in mind that what you enter will appear as part of the newsgroup for all to see.
3. Click on the **Send** button.

TIP: RESPONDING TO NEWS IN PRIVATE

If you want to respond to the person who has a newsgroup entry in private (as opposed to public), then click on the Re:Mail (not the Re:News) button and you can then send a private message.

Your response will then be posted in the same newsgroup, following the news article that you read and responded to. It won't appear immediately because it takes some time to travel from one computer to another. When you refresh the newsreader (by starting it over), you'll see your contribution. When you're done with news, just click on the icon in the upper left hand corner to close the window and return to the Netscape browser.

USING MAILING LISTS

There's another really neat way to use newsgroups. That's when you sign up for a listserv discussion group. A listserv discussion group is an automatic depository for information. If you subscribe to it, everything that the list receives, you receive as well. For example if you belong to the fat-free mailing list, each time someone sends mail to that list, you will receive it as well.

To subscribe to a mailing list, you need to provide the location of the list and a message telling the list administrator you want to subscribe. For example, here are the steps we would use to subscribe to the list containing recipes and an ongoing discussion about fat-free foods. All this is done in the e-mail program you use.

1. Type `fat-free-request@fatfree.com` in the **To:** field.
2. Type **subscribe** in the **subject** field and press **Enter**.

That's all there is to it. From then on, until you unsubscribe, you will receive a copy of everything that is sent to this list. Sometimes this can be one or two things a day, and sometimes it can be hundreds.

A WORD ABOUT FTP AND TELNET

FTP or file transfer protocol and Telnet are two useful tools. FTP allows you to transfer files from a remote location to your computer. Telnet allows you to operate another computer from a remote setting. There is one caveat, however.

With the onset of easy to use graphical Internet browsers such as Netscape, most files are available on a home page and you should not need to use ftp to transfer a file. You can just click on the filename. Same is true with telnet. You can just point your browser at the Library of Congress home page at `http://lcweb.loc.gov/` and then find whatever information you might need.

DOWNLOADING A FILE USING FTP

FTP is most useful to download files, including recipes and such. For example, to explore recipes of all kinds, type `ftp://ftp.neosoft.com/pub/rec.food.recipes/` in the Netscape browser **Location:** line and press **Enter**.

Here, you'll find thousands of recipes, and here's how a file was transferred from the Internet to my own computer.

1. I scrolled down to the cookie folder `cookies/` and double-clicked.
2. From the *30 brownie recipes* (!) I clicked on several until I found the one that I wanted. You'll find that recipe here.
3. Click on **File**, then click on **Save As** and save the file wherever you want on your hard drive.

RECIPE: BROWNIES

Here's another brownie recipe from the neosoft ftp site.

⅛ cup butter, melted
3 oz unsweetened baking chocolate (melt at very low temperature and allow to cool)
4 eggs
2 tsp salt
1 tsp vanilla
2 cups sugar
⅛ cup sifted cocoa powder
1 cup standard (plain) flour
2 cups chopped pecans

Beat the eggs until smooth and a little frothy. Add salt, vanilla, and the cooled melted chocolate and butter mix. Add sifted cocoa, flour, and pecans. Spread mixture into a greased 9 x 13-inch cake pan and bake at 350°F (180°C) for 25 to 30 minutes. There is no leavening agent, it's not a mistake. These brownies are especially nice if frozen after cutting into squares.

Telnet gives you the capability of controlling a computer from a remote setting. For example, you could go to the Library of Congress and see what holdings they have under the general heading of chocolate. To do this, enter `telnet://locis.loc.gov.` and press **Enter**.

You'll see the Library of Congress Information System (LOCIS), from which you can search for information about chocolate. You can see the results of the search below.

Telnet allows you to remotely access computers, so whatever is on the computer you access is information you can have. You probably won't be using the telnet tool often, because most sites now have home pages from which you can get the same information, but if you should run into it, you'll know what to do.

EVERYTHING YOU ALWAYS WANTED TO KNOW

Using America Online

•

Using the Compuserve Information Service

•

Using Microsoft Network

•

General Resources on the Internet

T *he Online Epicure* covers many different categories of food and food-related topics. If you're just starting out, however, it's best to become familiar with the more general locations on the big online services as well as the Internet. From any one of these locations, you can easily branch to others. In the following pages, you'll read about the major food locations on America Online, CompuServe, and the Microsoft Network, as well as home pages (from the Internet) galore. We'll also show the fundamentals of how to use any of the major online services in 5 minutes or less.

USING AMERICA ONLINE

AMERICA ONLINE IN 5 MINUTES

To send mail
1. Click on Mail Center.
2. Click on Compose Mail.
3. Type the address of the person to whom you want to send mail.
4. Type a subject.
5. Compose the message.
6. Click on Send.

To read mail
1. Click on Read New Mail.
2. Double-click on the mail message you want to read.

To reply to mail
1. Highlight the message you want to read.
2. Click on Read.

To access the Internet
1. Go to the Channels screen.
2. Click on the Internet Connection button.

To search for food-related sights
1. Go to the Channels screen.
2. Click on the Find button.
3. Type food.
4. Click on Search.

To create a Favorite Place
1. Go to the location you want to save as a Favorite Place.
2. Click on the Favorite Places icon.

To go to a Favorite Place
1. Click on the Favorite Places icon.
2. Click on the Favorite Place to which you want to go.
or
1. Click on GoTo, click on Favorite Places, then click on the Favorite Place to which you want to go.

To read a message
1. Go to the Message Board icon.
2. Click on Find New.
3. Read the new messages left since your last visit.

To enter a forum
1. Click on the Forum icon.

To add a message to a topic
1. Click on the Post Message button at the bottom of the window.
2. Type the subject and contents of the message.
3. Click on Post.

To create a new topic
1. Click on the Create Topic button.
2. Post your message in the new folder that is automatically created.

America Online is the largest of all the online services and offers a large collection of food-related sites. The easiest way to navigate is through the use of keywords such as food, cooking, and eating out. For example, you can begin with the keyword *food*, which reveals the Everything Edible! Window you see here containing links to the following areas:

AOL Cookbook	Health Diets
Bed & Breakfast Recipes	Jewish Community Food
BrewBase	Marketplace Food Area
DineBase	Review a Restaurant
Dining Companions	Sunset Magazine
Food, Fitness, & Travel	Vegetarians Online
Good Morning America Recipes	WineBase

On the same screen, you can access The Cooking Club, the Food & Drink Network, the electronic Gourmet Guide (known around the Internet as eGG), and *Woman's Day* Cooking. You can also click on the Web Sites button and America Online will show you what food-related Web sites it has indexed. You can then click on any one of those (such as Coffee Web Sites or Ben and Jerry's

Homemade, Inc.) and examine the home page. We'll examine all these sites and more when we focus on particular foods and related areas later on.

The keywords eating out take you to a collection of sites dealing with the restaurant community, including live chats and information, restaurant reviews, and *Restaurant Hospitality Magazine.*

Besides using e-mail in the traditional way to keep contact with individuals, America Online offers message boards. It's America Online's community access system, where more than one person can participate in a discussion. A message board (sometimes called a discussion board) is part of a forum, and many of the various cooking forums lead to message boards such as you see below for the America Online Cookbook. Once in a message board, you're welcome to list the categories (such as Breads, Pasta & Grains, and Low Fat/No Fat) in that board and browse. Each category contains topics, and each topic contains the messages that people contribute. Once you double-click on a category you like, then just browse or post a message of your own.

When you first start, just browse for a while so you can get some idea of the tone of other people's messages and the content as well. This will help give you some ideas about leaving messages of your own. Once you add a message, you'll find responses to that message the next time you open that message board.

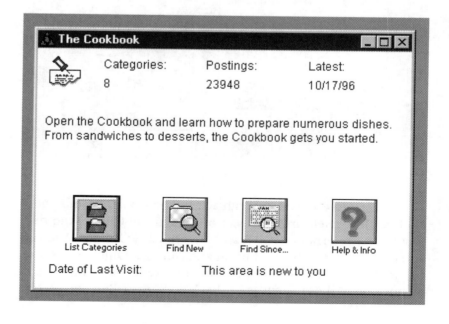

USING THE COMPUSERVE INFORMATION SERVICE

COMPUSERVE IN 5 MINUTES

To send mail
1. Click on Mail, then click on Create/Send Mail.
2. Enter the address of the person to whom you want to send mail
3. Click on OK.
4. Compose the message
5. Click on the Send Now button.

To read mail
1. Click on Get New Mail.
2. Double-click on the mail message.

To reply to mail
1. Click on the Reply button.
2. Compose the message.
3. Click on Send Now.

To search for food-related sights
1. Click on the Find button.
2. Type food.
3. Click on OK.

To access the Internet
1. Click on the Internet button.

To create a Favorite Place
1. Click on Services, then click on Favorite Places.
2. Click on Add.
3. Enter a description of the Favorite Place and the service name.
4. Click on OK.

To go to a Favorite Place
1. Click on the Favorite Places icon.
2. Double-click on the Favorite Place to which you want to go.

To join a forum
1. Click on Services, then click on Go.
2. Enter the name of the forum.
3. Click on OK.

To create a message in a forum
1. Click on the Create Message icon.
2. Enter the subject of the message.
3. Select the forum where you want the subject posted.
4. Type all in the To: text box.
5. Enter the message.
6. Click on Send.

To search for a message in a forum or a file in a library
1. Click on Messages, then click on Search Message.
2. Enter some keywords for the message.
3. Click on Search.

CompuServe is organized by forums, which are very easy to use. They consist of a library containing files dealing with an interest such as recipes or tips, and messages that represent communications between forum members.

When you enter a forum, keep in mind that each one represents the ongoing interaction between forum members. However, what you see in a forum today may not be there tomorrow. If you send a message and contribute to a forum, your contribution will appear, but it will probably not remain on the forum for long. Messages are constantly being scrolled off the forum by the forum administrator to make room for new messages, so be sure to frequently check for a response to your message.

THE BEST PLACE TO START:
THE COOKS ONLINE FORUM (GO WORD: COOKS)

The Cooks Online Forum you see here is the most comprehensive central location for information about food and related resources on CompuServe. As with other forums, you can join a conference (if one is in progress), download information from the Library, or interact with other CompuServe members by leaving a message.

WHAT'S IN THE COOKS ONLINE LIBRARY

The Cooks Online Library contains 21 different sections, each one containing files that are easily downloaded to your computer.

Here's a brief description of each. The Cooks Online Forum is the central location for information about cooking on CompuServe, and to get there, you need only type **Ctrl+G** and the keyword "cooks."

- General/System Help provides you with general information about the forum and serves as a location for suggestions, ideas, tips, and so on that don't belong in any other section. Look here first to become familiar with what Cooks Online has to offer and ideas that might be helpful. There's also help here on how to use the forums such as advice on using WinZip, a file compression program.

- New Uploads contains files that have been uploaded to the Library. These files remain new for 30 days and then are stored in the appropriate library so that they are easy to locate and download. For example, if you have a new recipe you want to share by placing it in a library section, it will appear here when you first upload it. Here you can see a small sample of some of the newest entries to the library. I tried Merilee's Triple-Decker Brownies—you won't be disappointed if you do the same.

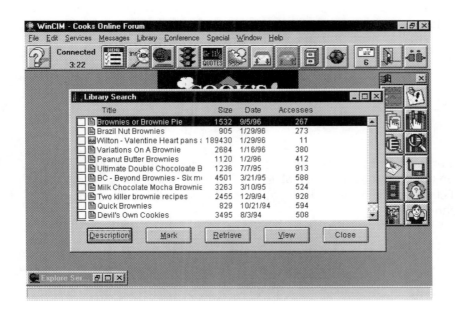

RECIPE: MERILEE'S TRIPLE-DECKER BROWNIES

Merilee says, "Although there are scads of brownie recipes already in the libraries, here is one more. Back when I was in high school, this was the gang's favorite treat, made by Merilee Maycock, one of our youth advisors. I made these a few weeks ago, here in England as my husband likes them (and he hates desserts). At least a third of them were passed over the garden fence to our next-door neighbor who loved them!"

Preheat oven to 350°F (180°C)
Bottom Layer
¾ cup flour
¼ tsp baking soda
¼ tsp salt
1½ cups rolled oats
¾ cup brown sugar
¾ cup melted margarine

Combine flour, salt and soda in a bowl. Add the rest of the ingredients and mix until well blended. Press into the bottom of a 9 x 13-inch pan. Bake for 10 minutes.

Second Layer
1 box brownie mix, prepared to cakelike variety
Spoon prepared brownie mix on top of bottom layer. Bake for 35 to 40 minutes, or until tester comes out fairly clean.

Third Layer
1½ oz unsweetened chocolate
3 tbsp butter
2¼ cups powdered sugar
1½ tsp vanilla
3 tbsp hot water

Melt chocolate and butter together in a large pan. Add the other ingredients and beat until well blended. Spread on top of the second layer while it is still hot. Cool until just warm, then mark into squares and cut. Sometimes if you let it get too cold before slicing, the bottom layer can stick to the pan a little.

- Holiday Fare provides you with recipes and ideas for making the holiday more enjoyable and less stressful. For example, Make Ahead Holiday Recipes provides those foods that will keep and reduce some of the last-minute duties you need to attend to during a holiday party.
- Trying to lose weight? Stay away from the Desserts and Sweets section, a select of goodies for after dinner. The No Bake recipes must be popular, because they've been downloaded almost 200 times in the last few weeks.
- Recipes and tips for preparing wild game, fish, and all types of poultry and meats can be found in the Meat, Poultry, and Fish section: Florentine Chicken, Veal and Peppers, Beef Hash, and the recent recipes from the *Miami Herald*—all at your fingertips.
- The Ethnic Recipes section is one of the most visited and popular, with ethnic dishes that can be identified with any ethnic group. Chris Frederick's recipe for Cajun Chicken served over linguini must be a hit because it had been downloaded almost 600 times in the month when I looked at it.
- If you're cooking over the barby or on a hiking trip, be it hamburgers or trout, stop at the Outdoor Cooking Library to find what you need to know about cooking outdoors. You'll find advice on just about everything here to do with barbecues including the perennial discussion over charcoal versus gas grills.
- Breads deals with breads, muffins, biscuits, pizza crusts, soft pretzels, and all the other wonderful things that come from the bread family.
- Microwave Cooking offers information about the convenience of microwave cooking.
- Vegetables—green and otherwise, for the nonvegetarian.
- Salads & Dressings—Here you will find an amazing collection of recipes for all types of dressings and a wonderful collection of salad recipes.
- Dining Out offers information on restaurants throughout the country.
- Healthy eating and good eating can go well together, as you can see in the Nutrition Meal-Planning and Nutrition library.

- Tools and Books brings you information on anything that might make cooking more enjoyable including cookbooks, products, and more.
- Magazines Online is where you will find online magazines that are participating in the forum—all types of magazines that have anything to do with food and nutrition. You can find ordering information as well as special events and offerings.
- Chicken soup for the soul and the tummy are found under Soups & Sauces along with the traditional and new recipes for soups and sauces.
- Egg/Cheese/Casseroles has recipes that we all love consisting of eggs, cheese, or eggs and cheese. Who doesn't love a good casserole on occasion?
- Food Professionals & Culinary Schools provides information about further education, both formal and otherwise.
- Pizza & Pastas of all shapes and sizes are found in this CompuServe library.

If you want to see how what you cook should look, see Visual Recipes.

USING THE FIND FEATURE IN COMPUSERVE

The best way to start getting information on any topic (such as food) in CompuServe, is through the use of the **Find** feature. Clicking on the **Find** button or selecting **Find** from the Services menu provides you with the dialog box you see below. You can see that we've already entered food for searching.

Searching for *food* results in the following list of forums and other related sites.

1-800-FLOWERS
Adventures in Food (Free)
Bacchus Wine Forum
Better Homes Kitchen Forum
Breton Harbor Gifts (Free)
Chef's Catalog (Free)
Coffee Anyone? (Free)
Consumer Forum
Cooks Online Forum
Dinner On Us (Free)
Exegete Restaurant Guide
Florida Fruit Shippers (Free)

Good Pub Guide
Health & Fitness Forum
Health Database Plus ($)
Honey Baked Ham (Free)
Inquest ($)
Liquor By Wire (Free)
Native's Guide to NY Forum
Natural Medicine Forum
Omaha Steaks Intl.
The Electronic Mall (Free)
The Gift Sender (Free)
Vegetarian

> Life is short, eat dessert first.
> —Unknown

You are not charged extra for using any CompuServe service unless it is followed by a $ such as the Health Database Plus as you see on the list. Also, those CompuServe listings followed by the word "Free" means you are not charged for your online time.

USING MICROSOFT NETWORK

The Microsoft Network is the newest of the major online services and like CompuServe is organized by forums. Once you are in a forum, you can open a folder (such as Recipes), post your own contributions, and reply to other people's contributions. The most basic unit of communication in the Microsoft Network is the message, contained in a forum.

Using the Microsoft Network directory (Go word: *msn direct*), you can find what forums are available within the general cooking topics. You'll find the following list:

- Encyclopedia Cuisines
- Gourmet Gift Net, offering a wide variety of places to shop for food and food-related things on the Net
- ICNN Food & Beverage Center
- ICNN Nutrition Center

MICROSOFT NETWORK TIP

To find the Go word for any area on Microsoft Network, right-click on the icon that represents the areas, click on Properties, and read the Go word in the Properties dialog box.

MICROSOFT NETWORK IN 5 MINUTES

To send mail
1. Click on E-mail in Microsoft Network Central.
2. Click on the New Message icon.
3. Type the address of the person to whom you want to send the mail.
4. Type a subject.
5. Compose the message.
6. Click on the Send icon.

To read mail
1. Double-click on the message you want to read.

To reply to mail
1. Click on the Reply to Sender icon.
2. Enter the message you want to send.
3. Click on the Send icon.

To access the Internet
1. Click on the Internet Center link in the Microsoft Network window.

To search for food-related topics
1. Right-click on the Microsoft Network icon.
2. Click on Find.
3. Type food.
4. Click on Find Now.

To create a Favorite Place.
1. Go to the location you want to save as a favorite place.
2. Highlight the service or folder.
3. Click on File, them click on Add to Favorite Places.

To go to a Favorite Place
1. Right-click on the Microsoft Network icon, then click on Go to Favorite Places.
2. Click on the Favorite Place to which you want to go.

To read a message in a forum
1. Click on the Forum icon.
2. Click on the folder that contains messages.
3. Click on the message you want to read.

To add a message to a forum
1. Click on the Compose menu, then click on New Message.
2. Type the subject of the message.
3. Enter the message.
4. Click on the Post icon.

To respond to a message in a folder
1. Double-click on the message to which you want to respond.
2. Type the response.
3. Click on the BBS icon.

What's Cooking Online is the central location for food connections on the Microsoft Network and is the place to start. To get there, you can use the Microsoft Network's Go word, cook. Just right-click on the Microsoft Network icon in the lower right corner of the screen. Click on **Go To**, type "cook," and press **Enter**.

What's Cooking Online opens the door to valuable resources related to cooking and food, including Kitchen Table Talk, Cooking Chats (which take place on Saturday at 1A.M., Tuesday at 5P.M., and Wednesday at 4P.M.), Recipes, Fast & Easy (quick, good food), What's Cooking Info Center, Passions (such as chocolate and barbecue), and the Vegetarian subforum. There are also

several connections to other food-related resources such as
Dining with Ale & Lager and Renaissance Cooking.

If you want a listing about everything on the Microsoft
Network related to food, then right-click on the Microsoft Network
icon, click on **Find**, type "food," and then click on **Search**.

As you can see below, you'll find hundreds of food-related
sites of all types including Web sites, folders, files you can
download, and more. The same result occurs when you search
for the keyword "cook" in the **Find** dialog box—more sites than
you probably bargained for. Using **Find** is a great way to get
started cruising for what might be available on the Microsoft
Network. There's no organizational scheme to this list other than
alphabetical, so your best strategy might be to scroll through the
list and double-click on any resource you want to further explore.

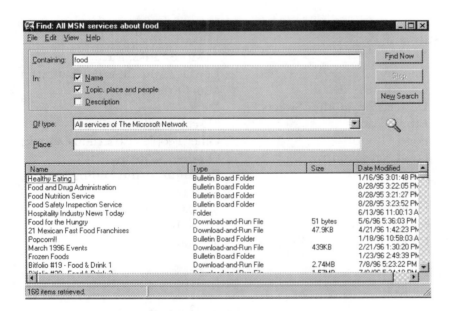

GENERAL RESOURCES ON THE INTERNET

The Internet is by far the richest source of information about
food online. Not only will you find recipes, reviews, interviews, tips
and tricks, and newsletters, but an extensive set of general pages

from which you can start your search. Here are some of the best starting points. These are just fun to go to and explore the links they've established with other location on the Internet. Are they all the great food pages? No. Is it a great place to start? Yes.

MIMI'S CYBER KITCHEN (http://www.cyber-kitchen.com/)

Mimi's Cyber Kitchen claims that it's the "best and largest food site of its kind on the world wide web." It might be hard to argue otherwise. With the Food Finder (for finding things about food on the Web), Recipe Request Line (need to make something out of figs and jalapeño peppers?), a hot recipe of the week, and an extensive collection of recipes in more than 25 categories, it's the place to start. Take a look at this list of links (including links to other people's links!), and you'll see why.

Beverages	Links To Recipes, Articles,
Bread	More Links, Etc.
Cheese	Lowfat (And Fat-Free) Eating
Chocolate!	Mail-Order Foods
Desserts And Other Sweets	Meat
Ethnic Foods	Miscellaneous
Food Humor	Other People's Collection Of Links
Food Newsgroups	Outdoor Cooking
Fruit	Restaurants And Dining Out
Health Foods	Seafood
Holidays	Spices/Condiments
Jewish/Kosher	Vegetables
Links To Sites With Recipes	Vegetarian

COOKING

(http://www.byu.edu/acd1/ed/InSci/Projects/uvpcug/cooking.htm)

It's fitting that this huge general page on cooking is named just that. This site contains over 100 links including dips, desserts, salads, sauces, fat-free archives, cookbooks, "ridiculously easy recipes," and even recipes from the lost dairies of Jean-Paul or the Iowa State University's insect recipes (cooking's cooking!).

COOKS' CORNER (http://wchat.on.ca/merlene/cook.htm#recipe)

Here's another incredible site full of wonderful resources. Lolli's menu (the title of this home page) is full of recipes (like Cranberry Chocolate Orange Cake), indulgences (chocolate, chocolate, and more chocolate and the like), coffee addresses, and loads of recipe sites.

KARIN'S COOKING STUFF (http://www.karinrex.com/cooking.html)

Karin Rex, Geeky Girl is how the title of this page reads, but don't judge a book or a Web site by its cover or its title. The new site is full of useful recipes (with more being added each month) and cooking links (along with a description of what the link contains) to some very good places such as Link Culinaire (The Professional Chef's Culinary Assistant, http://www.whytel.com/ftp/users/chefnet/), Cyber Recipes (http://www.cyberpages.com/RECIPE.HTM), and even the recipe for Grandma Anna's Chicken Soup should you feel under the weather.

FOODDAY (http://www.foodwine.com/food/foodday/)

What I like most about FoodDay is that it changes daily with a new presentation of a fresh recipe, tip, or some other food news that's informative and useful. You won't know in advance what's on the menu for that day, but it's worth the visit. The day that I visited, the subject was olives. After a discussion of cooking with olives and using olive oil, recipes for Smoked Salmon Rolls with Olive Cream Cheese and Spicy California Sicilian Style Olives were given, courtesy of Fred Rogers, the FoodDay author of the day. In addition to today's FoodDay, you can visit this site and go back and read any of the FoodDays from the previous year, a treasure of information. Now if they only published an index!

THE BLUE DIRECTORY (http://www.pvo.com/pvo/Food-Bev/)

This is one of those must-see stops. The Blue Directory of Foodservice Businesses contains categories and links to hundreds of other Web sites and is a great site to click and go from home page to home page.

For example, a click on **Coffee and Coffee Equipment** (under Non-Alcoholic Beverages) takes you to home pages for Jamaica Blue Mountain Coffee, Sovrana Trading Corporation, and two sites named Virtual Coffee (everything for the coffee lover). The categories seem to offer something for everyone; here's just a partial list:

Publications and References
Cookbooks
Magazines, E-zines and Guides
References and Resources

Food
Baked Goods
Cheeses, Fruits and Nuts
Grocers Online
Seafood
Meats
Kosher, and much more

To finish things off, Blue Directory contains a direct link to their bulletin board, where you can participate in discussions.

CHEFNET (http://www.chefnet.com/)

ChefNet started as a bulletin board for food service professionals, but is now full of all different types of information, much of it useful for the amateur as well. Message boards, newsletters, a listing of suppliers, jobs, and recipes—all make this a site that's chock full of food-related information. It's where professional chefs are most active on the Web.

You can receive additional information from the ChefNet people by registering, a simple process that takes only a minute or so. Because ChefNet is meant to cast a wide net, there are 12 different food categories such as Consumer, Chef/Operator, Average Citizen, Consultant, and Writer/Editor/Author. This is also the site where you can sign up for the Chef Celebration Tour (http://www.indianharvest.com/html/cheftour.html), visiting 20 major cities (such as Washington, D.C., Los Angeles, and Kansas City). At any one of these tours, you can watch great chefs perform their magic, learn tips, and earn three continuing education units (important to some of us!).

FOOD & WINE ONLINE (http://www.chefnet.com/wine/fwol13.html)

Food & Wine Online is the electronic version and update of the book of the same name by Gary Holleman, a chef who got a large part of the cyberfood movement started. He's the corporate chef at Indian Harvest, a supplier of specialty grains and legumes. This electronic newsletter contains links to food and wine sites, but also lots of information for food professionals including cooks, chefs, suppliers, and even snippets from interviews with famous chefs such as Julia Child.

FOODNET (http://www.foodnet.com/)

Another place for food service professionals and food-loving amateurs, FoodNet offers Consumer Editor (for use by magazine and newspaper food editors), Foodservice (designed for food service professionals such as chefs, cooks, and freelance food writers), and Food Bites (a taste of the FoodNet system for nonprofessionals). If you're a professional, you should register. If not, dive right into Foodbites, where you can get news about food, visit Foodtalk, click on Netlinks, or join the chef's table, a monthly feature which includes a famous chef and a link to one of his or her mouth-watering recipes, like the one shown on the following page.

EPICURIOUS FOOD (http://www.epicurious.com/a_home/a00_home/home.html)

You know you're on the right track when you see the Playing With Your Food link on this page. It may even be enough to convince you that you need not travel any further for fun, fun, and more fun.

This general food page is the primary link to *Bon Appétit* and *Gourmet* magazines as well as recipes, forums, and even a bit about travel. If you do want to play with your food, be sure to check out the Victual Reality site, where you'll find out why using the wrong glass for the right wine is tantamount to mixing water and chocolate, and other realities of the cooking world such as Julia Child's Hand and BonBons Away.

chef's table

Featured Chef of the Month

Leslie Revsin

Leslie Revsin

Chef Leslie Revsin's culinary style has been described by New York magazine as a "savvy blend of modern American and European." Gourmet magazine proclaims, "Once tasted, her dishes are usually not forgotten."

Leslie has chefed at many Manhattan's top restaurants including Bridge Cafe, One Fifth Avenue and Argenteuil. Most recently she was excutive chef at the Inn at Pound Ridge, Some 40 miles north of New York City.

After graduating magna cum laude from Macalester College in St. Paul, Minnesota, Lesie attended New York Technical College and received a degree in hotel and restaurant management. She began her career at the Waldorf Astoria Hotel as a "kitchen man" and rose to become its first woman chef in 1973. In 1977, she opened Resturant Leslie, her own nine-table bistro, in Greenwich Village.

Leslie starred in her own half-hour segment of the PBS series "Master Chefs of New York" and has made television appearances on other shows throughout the county.

Leslie Revsin has prepared a special dish for us this month
Angel Hair Pasta with Strawberry and Brown Sugar Sauce.

To Last Months Chefs Table

RECIPE: FILETTO DI MAIALE AL GORGONZOLA (GRILLED PORK LOIN WITH GORGONZOLA SAUCE)

Here's the August 1996 recipe from FoodNet

Serves 4
For the pork
4-4 oz pieces of pork loin denuded and cut ½-inch thick

For the marinade
¾ cup pure olive oil
¼ cup balsamic vinegar
1 tbsp honey
1 tbsp minced fresh marjoram
1 pinch white pepper

Emulsify olive oil with the rest of the ingredients and pour over the meat. Marinate for a minimum of 4 hours. Best if left overnight.

For pears
1 cup red wine (enough to cover pear)
⅓ cup dry marsala wine
½ each cinnamon stick
1 tsp vanilla extract
The peel of ½ lemon

Peel and core pear. Put pear in a small pot with all ingredients and cook until soft, but not mushy. Take pear out and reduce juices by half. Discard cinnamon stick and lemon peel, and reserve liquid.

For the sauce
Pear cooking juices
1 tbsp Gorgonzola dolcelatte
1 oz demi glaze

Assembly
Grill pork meat about 2 minutes on each side. Place sauce in a medium size sauté pan and grill meat. Finish cooking the pork in the sauce on one side only. Grill marks should be visible and not covered by the thick sauce. Cut pears in half and fan out for garnishing the plate. Pour sauce on the plate and place meat on top, drizzle some Gorgonzola and pieces of toasted walnuts on the pork. Serve dish with roasted new potatoes and lightly sautéed fresh vegetables.

EPICUREAN THYME (http://members.tripod.com/~Epicurean/index.html)

Don Zajac is the executive chef at the Flossmoor Country Club south of Chicago and put together this page. He offers a listing of almost 40 terrific links to other food-related sites, many of which we will cover in the pages to come. You can find information about Printer's Row Restaurants in Chicago, click to the Master Cook home page, try Ask the Chef, find out about the origin of certain culinary words (such as marmalade, originally from the Portuguese *marmelada* meaning "quince jam"), find where to get the hottest sauce on the Net, and more. If you're bored with all the links, you can always tell Don Z (the owner of the page) whether or not you like gorgonzola (the last question on his page!).

SYMPATICO: HOME & LEISURE: COOKING
(http://www1.sympatico.ca/Contents/Home+Leisure/cooking.html)

Here's an unusual collection of food-related sites including The Inquisitive Cook (cooking from a scientific perspective), FoodLines ("a meeting site for people who have passion for food"), The Virtual Kitchen (recipes and cookbook reviews), Ketchum Kitchen (cooks and tips), Specialized Cuisines (including vegetarian, Kosher, Italian, and garlic), and a collection of indices to other general cooking sites on the Internet. If that's not enough, there's also Fun Food, where you can learn how to roll your own sushi.

COOKING RAGU (http://www.ragu.com)

You cook because it's fun, and here's the Web site with the most built-in fun available. If you're interested in a site that's loads of fun and slanted toward Italian everything, than Ragu (also known as Mama Cucina) is it. You can have Mama Cucina send you new recipes as they are developed, enter a lookalike contest, and take a tour of Little Italy (that section of downtown New York full of wonderful *ristoranti* and where the famous San Gennaro festival is held each year).

JUMPING PAD (http://academy.bastad.se/~recipes/JumpingPad.html)

This is recipe central on the Web. Don't be shocked when you point to this site and find 21 pages (count 'em) of links for recipes from Medieval recipes, chocolate recipes, Disneyland's finest, and Yahoo's Ethnic Cooking page to recipe archives to Anna's place containing low-fat and low-calorie recipes. The page is not well organized, but if you want to do some digging, there are treasures to be found.

◄ RECIPES ►

Recipes on America Online
•
Recipes on Compuserve
•
Recipes on Microsoft Network
•
Recipes on the Internet

Walk into any cook's kitchen, and you're bound to find a book of recipes. Some of these cookbooks were gifts that are used for preparation of a special recipe. Others are the ones that are dog-eared and returned to over and over for that favorite waffle, cold tomato sauce, or eggplant appetizer formula. No matter how they're used, the relief of finding exactly what recipe is needed, when it is needed, is half the battle on the way to a great meal.

It's no surprise that you'll find thousands and thousands of recipes online. There are the general pages, the best of which we'll highlight, and then Asian, French, Jewish, Italian, and even sites that use insects. It takes all kinds.

All three online services offer collections of recipes, usually organized by type of food such as fruits and vegetables, meat and poultry, and breads.

RECIPES ON COMPUSERVE

Cooks Online and the *Better Homes and Gardens* forums are the locations on CompuServe where you will find recipes. Just browse through the libraries in these forums and you'll find a diverse collection of recipes that probably exceeds in number and variety what's available on America Online and the Microsoft Network.

The library in the Cooks Online forum is organized by food type. Double-clicking on any one of the categories in the Library list that follows reveals a list of recipes.

Holiday Fare	Fruits & Vegetables
Herbs and Spices	Salads & Dressings
Desserts and Sweets	Chile Pepper
Meat-Poultry-Fish	Potpourri
Ethnic Recipes	Soups & Sauces
Outdoor Cooking	Egg/Cheese/Casserole
Breads	Pizza & Pasta
Microwave Cooking	

You can see one such recipe here. Guess the Better Than Sex Cake is a hit, with more than 460 accesses, which means that it was downloaded that many times.

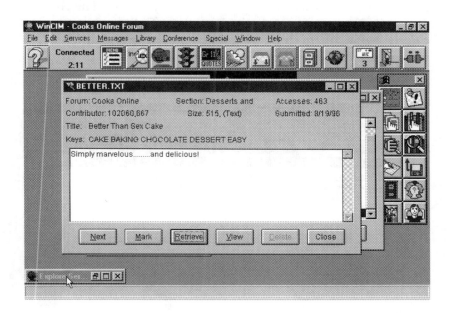

RECIPE: BETTER THAN SEX CAKE

Serves 10–12
1 box German chocolate cake mix
1 can sweetened condensed milk
1 jar caramel or butterscotch ice cream topping
1 (8-oz) container dairy topping, thawed
6 Heath bars, crushed

Bake cake in 9 x 13-inch pan according to package directions. When cool, poke holes all over cake with wooden spoon handle. Combine condensed milk and ice cream topping. Pour over cool cake. Refrigerate before spreading topping with dairy topping. Sprinkle crushed Heath bars over top of cake.

RECIPES ON AMERICA ONLINE

America Online offers two valuable sources of recipes: The *America Online Cookbook* and the *Woman's Day* section. The *America Online Cookbook* contains a limited number of categories, as you can see below, but each one seems to contain several different types of dishes. Here's what the options are.

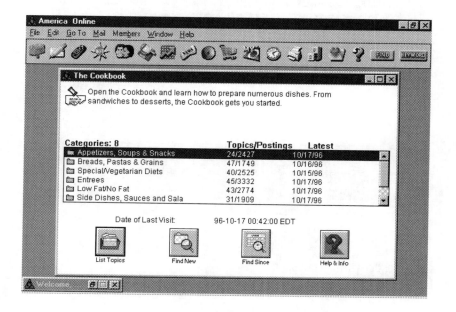

Appetizers, Soups & Snacks
Breads, Pastas & Grains
Low Fat/No Fat
Side Dishes, Sauces and Salads

Desserts & Sweet Treats
Entrees
Special/Vegetarian Diets
International Cuisine

These are all America Online bulletin boards, and double-clicking on any one reveals a listing of topics in that forum. From there, you can add a recipe, attach a posting (an electronic note) to another and so forth as we described earlier.

RECIPE

So many recipes are listed in the *America Online cookbook* that a new section of Mexican recipes had to be added to the Mexican Cookery category. Here's a recipe for a salsa, which has become an even more popular condiment than ketchup. Thanks to Nancy Mintz for this contribution to America Online.

Tomato Salsa
(serves 6 to 8) Time: 5 minutes preparation, 30 minutes soaking.
2 scallions (cleaned, 3 inches green left on, slivered lengthwise)
⅓ cup fresh lemon juice
½ cup cilantro (typically 2 bunches; use the leaves only)
2 garlic cloves, peeled and finely minced
¼ cup basil leaves, slivered
4 ripe plum tomatoes, seeded and cut into tiny dice
¼ cup purple onion, peeled and cut into tiny dice
1½ tsp ginger root, peeled and grated
1 tbsp balsamic vinegar
¼ cup olive oil
salt and white pepper

In a small bowl, soak scallions in lemon juice for 30 minutes. Drain scallions; reserve half of the lemon juice. Mince the scallions. In a medium-sized bowl, combine minced scallions, reserved lemon juice and remaining ingredients. Mix together well. Serve over grilled, broiled, or roasted chicken or fish.

The *Woman's Day* Online (keyword: *woman's*) area offers recipes in a series of areas categorized as well, including beef, chicken, pork, fish, vegetables, pasta, no-meat main dishes, dessert recipes, and quick dinners. They also offer a neat area that includes cooking tips, things we all can use once in a while, and a recipe finder. We entered turkey stuffing, clicked on **List Articles**, and found eight recipes and one entry for Sanity Saving meals (what an idea!).

TIPS

A Few Cooking Tricks from *Woman's Day* on America Online
- To check if an egg is fresh, place it in a bowl of salted cool water. If it sinks, it's fresh; if it floats, discard it.
- Meat marinades can be turned into delicious sauces. Just be sure to boil them for at least 3 minutes to kill any bacteria that may have been transferred from the raw meat.
- To reheat cooked rice, place it in a saucepan with 2 tablespoons of water per cup of rice. Cover and cook over very low heat about 5 minutes, or microwave in a covered bowl, 45 seconds to 1 minute per cup of rice, stirring occasionally.
- Drop tablespoonfuls of leftover canned tomato paste onto a waxed paper–lined baking sheet. Freeze uncovered until hard, then pack airtight and freeze up to 6 months. Add to soups, stews, or sauces.

RECIPES ON THE MICROSOFT NETWORK

There's no problem finding recipes on the Microsoft Network. Just right-click on the icon in the taskbar, click on **Find**, type "recipes," and click on **Search**. We found 48 locations on the Microsoft Network with information about recipes, but the best place to start is the main What's Cooking Online! folder and the Recipes option.

In folders organized by type of food you'll find the following categories in which you can investigate.

Appetizers, Dips, Salads	Pasta, Beans, Rice, Grains
Beverages (nonalcoholic)	Poultry
Bread, Biscuits, Muffins	Seafood
Eggs, Cheese	Side Dishes
Ethnic Specialties	Soups, Stews, Chowders, Sauces
Fruits, Desserts, Pastries	Special Diets
Holiday Foods and Info	Special Diets—Low fat
Meat	

Just to give you some idea of what's available within each of these categories, we found 205 conversations (all including recipes or commentary on recipes) in the Pasta, Beans, Rice, Grains area such as Bow Ties with Creamed Spinach, 10 different recipes for granola, Lasagna Rolls, and Pasta Primavera. Easy to find and easier to use.

The ICNN Personal Nutrition Center also offers recipes for very special populations such as adolescents, women, older people, athletes, and young children. Although these folders contain more than just recipes, the ample discussion of these topics as they relate to food and its preparation makes a visit worthwhile if you have concerns about nutrition for special populations. We'll cover nutrition online later.

RECIPES ON THE INTERNET

Finally, we get to the wealth of recipes available on various Web pages on the Internet. Once again, we're faced with the task of selecting those that are the best, and it would be hard to go wrong. There are hundreds if not thousands of home pages with information about recipes, and probably fifty of those deserve recognition. For now, we'll just pick those out that are unique, well designed, and allow you to get what you need fast. Then we'll move on to recipes for specific types of food.

START HERE

HOMEARTS RECIPE FINDER (http://homearts.com/waisform/recipe.htm)

Uh, oh. You need a vegetable side dish fast, and there's no time to surf the net to see what you can find. Turn to the Recipe Finder home page (see following page), click on the type of dish, the main ingredient, the calories per serving, and the preparation time, and even tell it how many recipes you want, and you're bound to find something. We wanted a pasta main dish, over 800 calories, that takes average prep time, and we got Pasta with Sausage and Broccoli Rabe. If you want, you can even enter an ingredient and search on that.

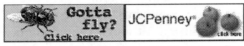

Recipe Finder

A recipe for every occasion!

search
talk to others
write to us
Eats

To find the recipe that meets your needs, choose from any of the following categories. Feel free to leave as many blanks as you like. Remember: The more elements you check, the more specific -- and limited -- your search results will be.

Type of Dish

☐ Appetizer
☐ Soup
☐ Main Dish
☐ Salad
☐ Desserts
☐ Snacks
☐ Side Dish
☐ Beverage

Main Ingredient

☐ Pasta
☐ Meats
☐ Poultry
☐ Fish
☐ Vegetables
☐ Rice & Grains
☐ Beans
☐ Leafy Green Vegetables
☐ Sweet or Savory Doughs
☐ Dairy
☐ Eggs
☐ Fruit

Calories per Serving

○ 0-200
○ 0-400
○ 0-600
○ 0-800
○ Over 800

Preparation Time

☐ Quick, 30 minutes or less
☐ Average, 30 minutes - 2 hours
☐ Long, over 2 hours

☐ Advanced Prep. - start at least a day in advance

Show me 40 ▾ recipes.

Type in any specific ingredient or other word you would like to find

[_____]   SEARCH!   CLEAR

REC.FOOD.RECIPES ARCHIVE

(http://www.ichef.com/rec-food-recipes/recipe-archive.html)

Here you see another "All you can ever want in recipes" page,
where you click on one category from a table of more than 25 and
select what you want. The only problem with this page is trying to
make up your mind from the hundreds of recipes that are
available. For example, in Candies & Snacks, you'll find well over
200 recipes, and in Barbeque you can count of around 150,
including Zen Barbecue Chicken and a variation of shish kebab
called Spiedies!

Table of Contents | Recipes | Tips 'n Hints | The Food Forum

I took the time to make availabe what I could find of the rec.food.recipes archive.
This archive will not be updated in the future. It will serve only as a basic resource
(albeit a useful one). All recipes contributed to The Internet Chef will be placed in the
Internet Chef Archive.

Search The Archive - *You can search the entire archive or by category!*

Appetizers	Barbeque	Beans & Grains	Beef & Veal	Beverages
Breads	Cakes	Candies & Snacks	Cookies	Desserts
Eggs & Dairy	Fish	Fruits	Miscellaneous	Pasta
Pies & Pastries	Pork & Lamb	Poultry	Preserving	Salads
Sandwiches	Sauces	Shellfish	Soups	Stews
Variety Meats	Vegetables			

The Pirch Script Page | Help on Scripting
Pre-Made Scripts

Member of the Internet Link Exchange

FOOD

(http://www-ssc.igpp.ucla.edu/~newbury/food.html#recipes)

The author of this page, Jenny Newbury, is a graduate student at UCLA and plans to run off to Australia and become a pastry chef if graduate school does not work out. Based on how much fun and how informative her Food page is, she certainly would be a success as a chef. Where many sites list categories of recipes, she lists her favorites such as Tomato, Saffron, and Roasted Garlic Soup, and Low-Fat, Stress-Free Cranberry Coconut Muffins. Almost as good as the recipes are some of the wonderful quotes included on her page.

RECIPES/DINING

(http://www.dibbs.net./points/recipes.html)

How about 80 links to recipes ranging from Ketchum Kitchen to Healthy Choice to Lobster Recipes? Love Hershey's chocolate syrup? Check out their home page. How about finding out who won the last 10 Pillsbury Bake Offs? You'll find that here as well. But most of all, you'll find a selection of recipes that are easily accessible and fun.

CENTRE POINT

(http://www.csquare.com/1110/food/cook.html)

Centre Point is a service that categorizes Web pages and includes Food as one of the major categories. Their ethnic recipes page has at least 60 links to other resources such as Australian recipes, Kusaya, Cajun Cooking, Turkish Cuisine, and New Mexican Recipes. It would be hard to find a culture that is not represented.

THE RECIPES FOLDER!

(http://english-www.hss.cmu.edu/recipes/)

Here's another general list of recipes organized by food such as Vegetarian Stuff, Dead Animals, and Things Possibly Involving Dead Animals and Possibly Not. A little bit of humor, sick or

---

> The best number for a dinner party is two: myself and a damn good headwaiter.
>
> —Nubar Gulbenkian

> Without butter, without eggs, there is no reason to come to France.
>
> —Paul Bocuse

> Let's get out of these wet clothes and into a dry martini.
>
> —Robert Benchley

otherwise, but a great page for a general overview of home pages. Many of these references refer to newsgroups such as rec.food.recipes. Click on the underlined link in the home page and you will go to the newsgroups area. Most browsers (such as Netscape) can easily transport you to the newsgroups of your choice. You have no need for a separate newsreader.

If you're an ethnic food fan, then go to the Ethnic Foods home page at http://www.cyber-kitchen.com/pgethnic.htm, 12 pages of ethnic foods under the general categories of Southeast Asian (Chinese, Japanese, Thai, Vietnamese, Singaporean, Filipino, Korean, Indonesian, Sri Lankan, Malaysian, and Balinese), Mexican (Mexican, Uruguayan, Chilean), Caribbean, Turkish and Russian, Middle Eastern/Mediterranean (Arab, Greek, Moroccan, and Persian), Indian, African, Creole/Cajun, American Regional, Canadian, Australian, and European (Belgian, British, Irish, French, and Italian). Anyone else hungry?

Sue's Recipe Server is also an ethnic food treasure house with a list of countries from which you select and then select a recipe from that listing. If you like, you can also view by category. So what are the top ten recipes off of Sue's Server? Traditional Pizza Dough, Salsa, Sesame Ginger Chicken, Pizza Capriciosa, Chicken Fajitas, American Crab Cakes, Caribbean Crab Cakes, Banffi Pie, Medium Balti Chicken, and Black Bean Chili with Avocado Salsa.

GO ITALIAN

(http://www.food.italynet.com/ricingl/defric/ricette.htm)

Feel like a Mold of Thrushes? Baked Ziti with Ricotta? How about Braised Fava Beans. Or, how about any one of 200 Italian recipes? You'll find them all here organized in alphabetical order, easy to locate and use on this link to Cucina Online and Italy Net. Not just food is featured, there's also kitchenware, events, and even news of the food world.

TARA'S RECIPE PAGE

(http://starburst.cbl.cees.edu/~tara/pastasalad.html)

Let's not forget the individuals who build and circulate their own home pages so that folks like you and I can take a advantage of their enthusiasm. Tara's page is one such site, and with recipes for Chocolate Peanut Butter Pie and Alsatian Onion Pie, visiting such sites should be a gustatory delight.

THE PUMPKIN PATCH COOKBOOK

(http://www.cc.gatech.edu/people/home/richb/cookbook.html)

As you will see later, quite a few cookbooks are advertised or mentioned online, but few offer the contents. *The Pumpkin Patch Cookbook* is the best organized and most informative online cookbook available (shown on the next page). A cursory look at the table of contents (all links that you can jump off from) shows you how complete it is. Don't shy away from these if you're not a pumpkin fan. The ingredient often adds moisture to recipes, much like other forms of squash, and does not necessarily overpower other flavors.

THE DINNER COOP

(http://dinnercoop.cs.cmu.edu/dinnercoop/)

We'll last mention a mother lode of over 600 recipes and 3,000 links to restaurants, shops, and other recipes! You'll find this at the Dinner Coop, an ambitious undertaking that allows you to search recipes and menus, and even by category of food. It's a complete food source and one that is worth visiting.

SPECIAL RECIPES

You just saw some of the best general sources for recipes, and now it's time to discuss the more specific sites that focus on particular types of food such as Italian, Asian, or Vegetarian. Here are a few great sites for different types of food.

Enter here, or scroll down to the index.

Go here if you missed my introduction and wanted to read it.
Go here if your browser doesn't support image maps.

Master Directory

Recipe Categories

Breakfast Recipes	Breads & Muffins	Bars & Cookies	Soups & Bisques
Side Dishes	Main Dishes	Dessert Recipes	Misc Recipes

Indexes

General Index	Lowfat & Nonfat	Lactose Intolerant	Vegan & Vegitarian

Appendices

Alternate Resources	Units & Conversions	Credits Page	Copyright Disclaimer

The Pumpkin Patch [last modified 09/19/96]

APPETIZERS

In the market for an appetizer? You would be well served to point your browser at Appetizer Recipes (http://godzilla.eecs.berkeley.edu/recipes/appetizers/) for 12 full pages of links to appetizers such as Cocktail Kebabs, Cranberry Cocktail Meatballs, Brie Crisps, Crisp Sugared Walnuts, Cavier Pie, Jalepeno Poppers, and Smoked Salmon with Brown Soda Bread. In addition, you can search on for a particular ingredient and find links to other recipes not on this extensive list. Our search for an appetizer made with tomatoes resulted in four pages of recipes. This is the mother of all appetizer recipe pages, and if you can't find anything for that opener here, it's time to order in.

Then there are the lists of actual recipes. These sites usually have less than 10 recipes listed, but they appear to be varied and well organized. A less ambitious Web page, also named Appetizer Recipes (http://foodnet.fic.ca/recipes/appet1.html), by the FoodNet people lists some interesting recipes such as Cheese Snacks, Mincemeat Balls, Cheddar Fondue, and Pakora (curried potato puffs). Another FoodNet page can be found at http://foodnet.fic.ca/recipes/appet2.html, and offers such appetizers as Honey Glazed Chicken Wings, Curried Turkey Pate, Liverwurst Rounds, Nippy Cheese Cubes, and Pork Cabbage Rolls with Creamy Mustard Sauce.

From Cooking with Caprial (http://www.pacificharbor.com/caprial/) there's a wonderful recipe for a favorite appetizer, Roasted Garlic. This is one of those simple and inexpensive starts that provides a stunning opener to a meal.

RECIPE: ROASTED GARLIC APPETIZER (FROM CAPRIAL, PBS CHEF EXTRAORDINARE)

To make the roasted garlic, cut off the top of a head of garlic, then place it in a roasting pan. Drizzle with a couple of tablespoons of olive oil and cover with a lid or foil. Place in a 325°F oven and bake 30 to 45 minutes or until the garlic is soft to the touch. Serve warm with a great mustard or a soft, mild goat cheese and sliced baguettes. Any leftover roasted garlic can be saved for pasta sauce or even soup.

You may think that caviar is expensive, and the Beluga at $400 for a ¼ pound may be, but you can get plenty of other types that have that same salty, rich taste. They just may not have the stamp of the Czar on the lid. If you are a caviar aficionado, take a look at Caviar (http://cybermal.com/caviar/cavrecip.htm), which lists 14 different appetizers from caviar, such as Hobo Salad, Eggs with Russian Caviar, and Beggar's Purses.

Vietnamese appetizers are not just for Asian-focused meals, but go well with almost anything. Vietconnection cooking (http://vietconnection.com/Arts/Aitems.map?39,105) offers a limited number of recipes, but you can find ones for spring rolls (http://vietconnection.com/Arts/cooking/recipes/Appetizer/Spring-Roll.htm) and egg rolls (http://vietconnection.com/Arts/cooking/recipes/Appetizer/eggrolls.htm). This is a good page from which to explore other Vietnamese food–related sites.

Here's a page without a title (http://www.shellcan.com/cmarket/appetiz.htm) that offers 12 appetizers, one for each province in Canada. They don't read as especially Canadian in nature or ethnicity (which who knows is what?), but they sure do sound delicious, especially such titles as Wild Mushroom Salad with Brown Vinaigrette, Phyllo Tourtiers with Onion Marmalade, and Roasted Blue and White Potatoes with Two Dips.

ASIAN

Our food tastes seem to change as a function of which national group has the largest emigration rate to the United States. These days, it's Asian, including Vietnamese, Indonesian, and others. With them come wonderful recipes that rely mostly on quick cooking with relatively little fat—a natural for these fast-paced times.

Cooking—Undiscovered Vietnamese (http://vietconnection.com/Arts/cooking/Cooking.htm) is a wonderful starting point for this combination of French and Chinese cooking. Not only can you link to recipes for salads (such as Green Papaya Salad), seafood (Fried Fish), poultry (Lemon Chicken), pork (Spare Ribs), rice, noodle soup (Pho Bo), and desserts (Yogurt), you can also find out about one of Hanoi's best restaurants (http://vietconnection.com/Cooking/CNews2/chaca.htm).

Maple Leaf Prime Chicken offers a few recipes at http://www.goprime.com/recipe/quick/ featuring Chicken Satay, Oriental

Chicken, and Amazu Chicken, but your best bet is to turn to Sue's recipe server at `http://www.hubcom.com/cgi-win/recipe.exe/1` or Ethnic Foods at `http://www.cyber-kitchen.com/pgethnic.htm` and click on the specific country. Additional Chinese recipes (`http://www.cs.cmu.edu/~mjw/recipes/ethnic/chinese/chinese.html`) and Japanese recipes (`http://www.twics.com/~robbs/tf-recp.html`) are also available.

BARBECUE

Does anyone not like b-b-q (or barbecue or barbeque)? It's probably un-American to do so, and just as un-American not to eat your favorite regional style, be it the spicy Kansas City sauce or the sweet rubbed Chicago version. As you might expect, the Web is full of barbecue recipes.

These home pages fall into two categories: favorite barbecue sauces and favorite barbecue sauces. Does that tell you anything? If you're looking for passion and enthusiasm, try these on for size.

Dave (Frary)'s cooking page at `http://www1.shore.net/~jdf/cooking.html` offers his "foolproof way to make tasty smoked & barbecued ribs," and prepares his pork ribs for about six hungry people. This is a 2-day deal where you mix and apply the rub 2 days before and then cook them the next day for at least 2 hours. Dave goes on to offer his Easy Roasted Chicken recipe (for gas grills), his favorite barbecue sauce, smoked fish, and smoked salmon marinade, and he ends with a list of recommended books.

Another Dave (McKeown) offers his recipe for pork ribs at `http://www.cs.cmu.edu/afs/cs/usr/maps/www/traditions/bbq.html`. This is a 2-day deal as well, where the ribs marinate for up to 24 hours and are then cooked as slowly as possible. At this same site you'll find recipes for Jamaican Jerk Baby-Back Ribs, No-Grill BBQ Brisket, and Hellfire Incineration Ribs. Visit this page—it's full of fun notes by the recipe authors and observations on life in general (such as "What's more important: your aorta or your taste buds?").

Great Recipes (`http://www.nottingham.com/barbecue/recipes.htm`) for smoking and grilling offers tips, secrets, and recipes including Brisket, Brisket Rub, Lemon Pepper Thyme Rub for Steaks and Burgers, and good information about using MSG in your recipes. This page has some great links for those interested in barbecue

TIPS

Here are some tips from the Great Recipes BBQ page.

- Use a good steel scraper or spatula often when using the cutting board. This will tend to keep the cutting board clean and sanitary. A steel brush will rough up the finish and should be avoided.
- Always cook more than you plan on eating that day. It freezes well and tastes great on those cold and rainy days when the weather really is too bad to barbecue. We realize the weather must really be threatening because very little stops the real barbecue chef!
- Have you placed the meat on the hot grill only to have it stick and pull apart when you try to turn it over? A simple remedy is to take a small amount of cooking oil and use a bristle brush to coat the surface lightly. This should reduce or eliminate most sticking to the cooking surface.
- Always remove as many of the ashes from your grill or smoker as possible. Although the ashes themselves pose no particular problem, the problem comes in when they become moist/damp/wet. When water combines with the ashes, it creates a very corrosive compound capable of eating through most anything. Your equipment will last much longer when properly taken care of.

including links to wood grilling, gas grilling, barbecue tips, tools, specialty woods, water smokers, and a schedule of cookoffs.

There are also links to Basting and Marinades and Dry Rub pages with more recipes, and of course there are the sauces, for which there are singular home pages such as Anna's (http://www.culinaria.com/freeaccess/catalog1/a/annasBarbecueSauce.html), using bottled meat concentrate; Sybil Carter's (http://ichef.cycor.ca/bbq/recipes/sauce/7219.html), which uses bacon and vinegar; and of course, the greatest barbecue sauce in the nation at http://www.barbeque.com/champs/, from the Kansas City Barbecue Society. These are commercial products, but the page is a good one because it leads you to a list of festivals and contests and is a source for ingredients.

BEVERAGES

There's not a whole lot about beverages on the Net, but there is one gem: the Epicurious Drinking home page at (http://www.epicurious.com/d_drinking/d00_home/drinking.html). This is where you want to go to find The Drink File, which contains hundreds of recipes, a drinking dictionary, and even tips about toasting.

You can also find a nice selection of what's available through The Internet Mall: Food & Beverages. There's a listing of companies supplying beverages including coffee, tea, beer and alcoholic, and nonalcoholic beverages, as well as suppliers of beverage-related items such as glassware. You can even order the recipes for 35 cordials that you can make yourself at Sweet Sips (http://www.mkt-place.com/sweetsips/cthomas.html).

Flora's Recipe Hideout (http://www.deter.com/flora/mxp/drinks/279.html) offers some alcoholic drinks such as Sex on the Beach and Ruby Punch Bowl, and you'll find a great home page for alcoholic drinks at http://www.TheVirtualBar.com/, as you see on the next page. It might not be summer when you read this, but the Lipton Tea folks (http://www.lipton.com/june-bev.html) provide some very nice and cool iced tea drinks such as Citrus Sun Tea Cooler or Tropical Delight.

DESSERTS

"Life is short, eat dessert first." That's what's on my kitchen door, and it's why our family always starts the buffet line *at the end* to be sure to get all the good desserts first! The Desserts home page features every imaginable sweet from a simple sugar cookie to the most complex of tower desserts. Let me caution you that the serious chocolate eaters should go to the chapter on chocolate, because chocolate deserves coverage in its own right.

Start with Desserts & Jam Recipes (http://www.commisso.com/recipe/dessert.html) from the Commisso Food Market where there are some 20 different recipes for delights such as Chocolate-Glazed Pear Tart, English Toffee Bars, and Rhubarb Jam. Each recipe is laid out in a table (such as you see here), making it easy to assemble the ingredients. The recipe steps follow the list of ingredients. There's also an interesting set of recipes made with Angostura bitters that can be found at http://www.caribinfo.com/angostura/angosdes.html. Grandma's Pumpkin Pie, Chocolate Mousse, Bread and Butter Coconut Pudding, and Crème Caramel Angostura are only some offered. In case you don't know, Angostura is the brand name for a secret (since 1824) combination of herbs and spices used to flavor and season food.

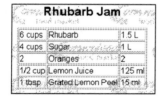

Rhubarb Jam

6 cups	Rhubarb	1.5 L
4 cups	Sugar	1 L
2	Oranges	2
1/2 cup	Lemon Juice	125 ml
1 tbsp	Grated Lemon Peel	15 ml

 THE VIRTUAL BAR

Recipe Retriever — | Alphabetic Listing | Listing By Ingredient | Listing Drink

What's New
The latest news and info

Corky's Jukebox
A large collection of midis

Bar Tips & Secrets
Silly Tricks and more

Stocking Your Bar
What you need to succeed

Brand Names
Popular liquor brand names

Liquor Information
A glossary of terms

Glasses
All about glassware

Utensils
Get the right tools

Toasts & Toasting
Cheers for all occasions

Submit a recipe
Add your favorite drink

Drinking Games
Corky's extensive collection

Silly Little Bar Tricks
Some silly little bar tricks to play

Corky's Game Room
Darts, Pool, etc.

Feedback
Send us your comments

Corky's Favorite Links
Industry-related links

About the Authors
Willie, Tiny and Dan

I'm Corky
Would you like a tour?

We've Got Cookies!

LINKZ.COM

THE BAR

Welcome to the Tour!

It's easy and fun to learn how to navigate through the Virtual Bar. In no time at all you will be searching for drink recipes, mixing drinks, listening to music and learning about all kinds of weird stuff. This site is useful because it gives you the ability to search Corky's 2,200+ and growing drink database in a variety of ways.

The most popular way to search is the Alphabetic Listing. It is frame enhanced and is considered to be the power users page. All search methods can be performed from this page. If you want more power this is where you want to be!

In addition to the alpha listing, there are several other ways to search Corky's database. You can perform a Query Search *(search by name or string)*, a Bar Stock Search *(search by ingredients you have on hand)*, a Drink-Type Search *(search by category, like shots)*, a By Ingredient Search *(search by particular ingredient)* or Corky can dish you up a Random Drink, or two, or ten, or 100. The graphic *tabs* at the top of every screen allow you to access the different search engines. No more fumbling through recipe books, downloading web page after web page of useless data or scanning through a huge drink list, Corky can help you find drinks quickly and easily.

But there's more to the Virtual Bar than drink recipes. . .

After you've found a great recipe, you might find Corky's Jukebox to be a nice diversion. You can listen to a variety of musical styles while you surf, mix or consume.

Just because you're in a virtual bar doesn't mean you can't enjoy some of your favorite bar games. You can goof off in the game room or challenge your friends to a drinking game. There is a bunch of information about liquor. You can learn useful bar tips and secrets, find out what glasses, utensils and ingredients you need to create the ultimate home bar.

Hi, I'm Corky! I will be your tour guide through the Virtual Bar. I'd like you to meet my friends. ENJOY!

TIP

Almost every large food company has a home page these days, and even if you haven't seen or been told about their home page, you can usually find it by typing *http://www.* before the name and *.com* after it, so if you want to know about Mars (makers of M&Ms), try `http://www.mars.com`.

Personal collections yield some nice recipes as well, such as Martha's Dessert Recipes at `http://www.esva.net/martha/dessert.htm` or Jame's Desserts Page (`http://www.science.uwaterloo.ca/~jharynuk/recipes.html`).

Once you're finished with the serious stuff, turn to the Mostly Desserts and Other Culinary Atrocities home page (`http://www.aus.xanadu.com/GlassWings/food/recipe.html`), where you'll find featured such delicacies as The Chocolate Biscuits of Doom, Fake Reese's Peanut Butter Cups, Hoptcha-cha Nachos and the ever popular Really Gross Over-Sweet Popcorn Balls.

FRENCH

Each day, all over France, almost everyone goes to the bakery for that day's supply of bread, so what would be more appropriate than for us to begin with recipes for that crusty, both tart and sweet, staple? For whatever reason, the Black & Decker (`http://www.blackanddecker.com/household/recipes/bread/french.shtml`) company offers an excellent recipe for classic French bread. It seems that tech companies are into baking, because an engineer from Hewlett-Packard (Bill Turner) has an equally good recipe (`http://www.ebicom.net/kitchen/page/sourdo/sdfrench.htm`).

After you try one of the hundreds of other recipes for French bread on the Net (use any search engine such as AltaVista or Excite), you'll need something to put it in. Try The French Bread Basket Company at `http://www.pnh.mv.net/ipusers/basketman/baskets/bb-2.htm`, a site ready to completely equip you for your next picnic.

Anchoïade? Tarte aux Courgette? Macaroni à la Niçoise? Pompe de Noël? These are just four of the recipes from Beyond the French Riviera (`http://www.beyond.fr/food/dishes.html`), the richest Internet site for recipes from a country where people drive very fast and eat very well. This site offers recipes for appetizers, vegetables, pasta, pizza, pastry, salads, sauces, and soups.

Another general page for French recipes is David Henderson's Page of French Recipes (http://jeffco.k12.co.us /dist_ed/spring96/onlinec/dahender/recipes.html) offering Appetizers, Soups, Entrees, and Desserts. David even included an interesting essay on French cooking that has links to some interesting and very useful French cooking sites such as Centrale Lyon (http://www.ec-lyon.fr/Home.en/Rhone-Alpes/Lyon/Art_de_ vivre/Cuisine/main.htm), featuring Paul Bocuse and a link to Secrets of Great French Chefs (http://users.aol.com/noisykids/ private/secrets3.htm). Just a few clicks from Dave's page is the monthly recipe from the French Culinary Institute in New York City (http://plaza.interport.net/fci/recipe.html). You can read more about the FCI in Chapter 16, "Cooking Classes and Schools."

ITALIAN

If you're going to Europe to eat, after your visit to Southern France, take a stop on the way home in Italy. If you can't get to Italy, try Mama Cucina's home page (www.ragu.com), which is full of recipes and fun, or try Italian Classics (http://www.wegmans. com/tonight/italy.html), which offers the list of categories you see on page 75, with more than 150 recipes. If you're really pressed for time, stick with Italian Classics and click on the **Dinner Tonight?** icon to find a recipe you can prepare in 30 minutes or less, for $4 or less per serving (not cheap!), using fewer than eight ingredients, and having less than 30 grams of fat per serving. This day's feature was Tuscany Shrimp with Sugar Snap Peas.

Other selections of Italian recipes are offered by the Mad Italian Chemist Scientist (http://www.mtech.edu/wwwclass/fboroni/ recipes.htm), where you'll find recipes for Bagna Cauda (a paste of garlic, butter, oil, and anchovies served as a dip) and Ravioli. Besides this entertaining Mad Scientist's recipes, there's an interesting offer for a pre-1930s recipe book titled My Italian Heritage (http://iaswww.com/fndraise.html), which also includes a coupon for a disk full of 500 other recipes.

RECIPE: NAVARIN AUX FIGUES ET FENOUIL—LAMB STEW WITH FIGS AND FENNEL

Recipe of the Month, from the restaurant of the French Culinary Institute.

For the lamb
½ cup vegetable oil
2 lb lamb shoulder, boned and cut into 1-inch cubes
salt and pepper
1 onion, peeled, diced
1 carrot, peeled, diced
2 stalks celery, diced
1 tbsp tomato paste
2 tbsp flour
6 cups lamb or veal stock, heated
2 tomatoes, coarsely chopped
3 cloves garlic, peeled, crushed
Bouquet garni (bay leaf, thyme, parsley, peppercorns wrapped and tied in a leek leaf)

For the fennel and figs
¼ cup olive oil
2 bulbs fennel, quartered
8 fresh figs, halved
1–2 tbsp chopped tarragon

1. For the lamb, heat the oil in a braising dish until very hot.
2. Season lamb with salt and pepper and add to hot oil. Sear on all sides, then remove.
3. Add onion and carrot. Sauté until caramelized. Add celery, sauté until softened.
4. Add tomato paste, sauté two minutes.
5. Add flour and mix into the fat.
6. Return lamb to the pan and cover with stock.
7. Add tomatoes, garlic, and bouquet garni. Braise in a 350°F oven for one hour or until meat is very tender.
8. Remove pan from the oven, strain the sauce into a sauce pan, and keep warm. Add lamb pieces back to braising dish.
9. For the fennel and fig, heat olive oil in a saucepan.
10. Add fennel and cook over medium high heat until well browned. Reduce heat and cook 10 minutes longer to soften.
11. Add figs and tarragon. Cook another 5 minutes.

To serve, place a few lamb pieces in a shallow-rimmed serving bowl. Drape a few pieces of fennel and several figs on top of the meat and spoon sauce over all.

Our Italian Classics products shine in these recipes.

- Beef Recipes
- Chicken and Turkey Recipes
- Fish Recipes
- Pasta with Beef Recipes
- Pasta with Chicken Recipes
- Pasta with Seafood
- Pasta with Vegetables
- Pizza Recipes
- Polenta Recipes
- Pork Recipes
- Salad Recipes
- Sandwich Recipes
- Sausage Recipes
- Shellfish Recipes
- Soup and Stew Recipes

Dinner Tonight?

Italian Classics Cupboard

Wegmans

Guestbook

Who doesn't associate Italian with pasta? The Pasta home page (http://www.food.italynet.com/pasta/default1.htm) allows you to finally find out what all those names of different pasta you see in cookbooks (like crespelle, taconelle, and trife) are and what they look like. Finally, it looks like the people at Black & Decker are up to it again. You can find their recipe for Italian bread at http://www.blackanddecker.com/household/recipes/bread/italian.shtml.

RECIPE: TROFIE

This twisted gnocchi is a specialty from Liguria. Mix together 1 lb of flour, 3½ oz of bran, a pinch of salt, and water. Knead the mass to obtain a smooth, compact, and elastic ball of dough. Roll to 1 inch thick and cut into 3 strips. Pinch off pieces of pasta the size of a chick-pea and, with the palm of your hand, rub them across the pastry board one at a time forming elongated twisted gnocchi about 1½ to 2 inches long. Trofie are cooked in plenty of boiling, salted water together with a finely sliced potato and a handful of very thin string beans cut 1-inch long, and served with pesto. The cooking time is 10 minutes.

JEWISH

For whatever reason, there are loads of recipes that fall under the general category of "Jewish" on the Internet. Perhaps that's because there are so many celebrations in that cultural tradition, all including food of one sort or another. As with any large number of home pages, when you use a search engine, search as specifically as you can. Rather than using the general keywords "Jewish food," try the holiday, such as "Passover recipes" or the specific food, such as "potato latkes." Keep in mind that the majority of recipes on the Net are holiday recipes, so be sure to read "Holiday and Festival Foods." Also keep in mind that around holiday time, there will be an increase in the number of recipes that are available.

A great place to start is the Kosher Express (http://www.marketnet.com/kosher/recipes.html), which lists recipes for holidays such as Passover and the High Holidays, but also has links to other sites including the Jewish Food Recipes Archives (http://www.eskimo.com/~jefffree/recipes/). Here you send an e-mail message with the word "subscribe" in the subject line to jewish-food-request@eskimo.com and you will receive recipes, restaurant reviews, and more on a regular basis (at no charge).

Another terrific source is the Jewish Recipes (http://soar.berkeley.edu/recipes/ethnic/jewish/), part of the Searchable Online Archive of Recipes, or Soar (at http://godzilla.eecs.berkeley.edu/recipes/), which includes a ton of wonderful recipes, many of them new. Here you'll find the old favorites such as Knishes and Strudel, and also new ideas based on old tastes such as Herring in Cherry Tomatoes or Russian Potato and Mushroom Croquettes. Phillip Goldwasser (http://www.jcn18.com/food/) lists recipes, many for Passover and others for Shabbat (the Jewish Sabbath).

Finally, there's Yale University's link to the middle east (http://www.cs.yale.edu/homes/hupfer/global/regions/mideast.html#israel), where you click on the country you're interested in learning about. In this case, we clicked on Israel and found 10 links to sites for Jewish food, including some already mentioned here and others that contain valuable and entertaining information such as Ethiopian Jewish Food and Recipes (http://www.cais.com/nacoej/

RECIPE

Here's Phillip Goldwasser's Basic Kugel recipe.

6 medium potatoes
1 onion
2 eggs beaten
⅛ cup matzoh meal
¼ tsp baking powder
Salt & pepper

1. Peel the potatoes. Place in cold water to keep them from changing color while you peel the rest. Then grate the potatoes and put in large bowl.
2. Chop the onion and mix in with the potatoes.
3. Add the rest of the of the ingredients and mix well.
4. Salt and pepper to taste.
5. Prepare a glass 8 x 8-inch baking dish with nonstick spray.
7. Pour mixture into baking dish and place in a preheated 350F oven for 25 to 30 minutes until the top begins to turn brown.
8. Let stand 5 minutes before serving.

13.html) and Yiddish Recipe Archives (ftp://sunsite.unc.edu/pub/ academic/languages/yiddish/recipes/) which offers everything from hamantashcen (served on Purim) to, you guessed it, more kugel!

Then of course, everyone has their favorite recipes be it for latkes (fried potato pancakes, http://ichef.cycor.ca/rec-food-recipes/vegetables/latkes02.html), kugel and coffee cake (http://www.jewish.com/bk951110/cook.htm), and more kugel (http://www.jcn18.com/food/bt6.htm) from Phillip Goldwasser.

There is also an especially nice selection of books about Jewish or Yiddish cuisine. You can find sample contents of several such as *Yiddish Cuisine: A Gourmet's Approach to Jewish Cooking* by Robert Sternberg (http://www.aronson.com/Judaica/ yidcook.html), Joan Nathan's wonderful new book, *Jewish Cooking in America* (http://www.randomhouse.com/special/ passover/tastes.html), and *Jewish Cooking from Here and Far* (http://www.rockower.com/ cookbook.htm) from the Beth Israel Congregation in Carmel, California, the winner of several cookbook awards. They even offer a sample of the recipes that are contained in the cookbook.

NATIVE AMERICAN

Native Americans gave the settlers corn, and it's no surprise that this formed a staple of the North American Indian diet. It also shows up in the majority of Native American and Native recipes you find on the Internet. All the pages here are the work of Paula Giese, an obviously devoted cook of, and expert on, Native American foods.

A whopping 10 pages of recipes (`http://indy4.fdl.cc.mn.us/~isk/food/recipes.html`) lists wiisiniwan (loosely translated by Paula Giese as "skill or talent for making food good to eat") beginning with Fry Bread, then Wild Rice, Maple (as in sugar candy and Quick Maple Upside Down Pudding), Corn (such as Posole, a Southwestern stew using hominy), Beans and Greens, Squash, Deer Meat, and Fruits and Berries (such as Wajape, traditional Lakota berry pudding). Not all the recipes are North American in origin. There are recipes for Xocatl (chocolate) from Central American groups such as descendants of the Aztecs and Mayans and information on Native food cookbooks and online bookstores.

Did you know that cocoa beans used to be used for money, and that 100 of them would buy a slave (in the time of Cortez)? Chocolate might not be as valuable now, but people still love it and early Central American recipes such as Mayan Hot Chocolate and Molo Roje for turkey or chicken are different, adventurous and interesting. You can find them all at `http://indy4.fdl.cc.mn.us/~isk/food/r_choc.html`, also by Paula Giese. Chocolate on chicken? Mole sauces are not sweet, but like any good sauce, enhance the flavor of what they accompany.

RECIPE: ROAST NEW CORN ON THE COB FOR (OUTDOOR) POWWOW

The key to this is fresh corn from the field just that morning trucked in to the powwow ground before noon. Cut it with an 8-inch stem attached to the cob. Make a big bed of coals with a grill over it that has removable pieces so you can keep adding wood or charcoal through the afternoon. Collect several big tin gallon cans to hold melted butter to dip the roasted ears in and big plastic garbage bags for the discarded husks. Pull the husks down and strip off some silk and remove any worms. Pull the husks back up, and put the ear on the grill. Turn it a couple times. Usually after about 7 to 10 minutes it's done, but this varies with the type of corn (and freshness). The husks should blacken slightly at their edges, but not turn brown. Push the done ears off the direct heat. When serving, pull off the husks (into the compost!) and dip the ear into melted butter.

QUICK COOKING

Everybody seems to be in such a hurry, among the fastest growing entries on recipe pages are those that can be made in 30 minutes or less. Quick doesn't mean unhealthy. Supermarkets are catering to busy lifestyles with prechopped ingredients, so with a bit of time, some creativity, and a visit to the home pages that follow, you'll have dinner on the table in no time.

There's no recipe for bread that takes only a few minutes, and the "quick breads" moniker at `http://ichef.cycor.ca/rec-food-recipes/breads/quick/quick.html` only means they don't take a long time to rise. This home page offers recipes for more than 80 different quick breads from Broccoli Cornbread to English Crumpets to Scottish Oatcakes.

Quick recipes also turn up from Maple Leaf Prime Chicken (`http://www.goprime.com/recipe/quick/`), Quick Recipes (`http://vd1.magibox.net/recipes/html/quick_recipes.html`), and contributions from the most beleaguered of chefs—parents who have hungry children standing by the stove asking "Is it soup yet?" (`http://www.parentsplace.com/readroom/recipes/recipes.html`). What's especially nice about this last URL, named ParentsPlace.com, is that the user is invited to submit his or her own recipes and help build up the library of available quick recipes.

SOUPS AND SALADS

As with almost every recipe category we write about here, soups and salads on the Internet are the province of big pages that contain lots of alternatives. For example, at Comisso's Market (`http://www.commisso.com/recipe/salad.html`) you can find a Russian, a Vegetable, a Potato, and an Apple Cole Slaw salad. Then there are more bean salad recipes than you might want to know about, but if you really need that one salad to complete the luncheon for the Lady's Club, Bean Salad Recipes at `http://godzilla.eecs.berkeley.edu/recipes/bean-salads/` offers recipes for Two, Three, and Four Bean Salad as well as You've Got To Be Kidding bean salad (an interesting combination of red beans and spices such as fenugreek and coriander). Finally, FoodNet (`http://foodnet.fic.ca/recipes/salad.html`) offers an extensive collection of salad recipes broken down into four sections. It's not clear why these are divided into sections, but each one contains many different salads using a diverse set of ingredients.

It's the same with soup. There's Soup Recipes (http://www.cc.gatech.edu/people/home/richb/Pumpkin/soups.html), a collection of 20 different vegetarian soups made with pumpkin; the Homemade Soup Recipes page (http://www.loci.com/HO/living/issue13/soup.html), with such favorites as Senate Bean Soup (all that gas?), Tomato-Onion, Expandable Chicken, and Shrimp Chowder; and Wegman's Recipes (http://www.wegmans.com/kitchen/recipes/soups.html), featuring Cheesy Broccoli and Italian Wedding soups, all nicely presented in tabular format and easy to follow.

There are also the soup and salad recipes based on individual contributions such as a vegetarian pasta salad (http://starburst.cbl.cees.edu/~tara/pastasalad.html), Jenny's Shrimp Salad with Cilantro-Chili Dressing (http://www-ssc.igpp.ucla.edu/~newbury/recipes/shrimpsalad.html), Crab Salad (http://www.pwseafood.com/recipes/crsalad.htm), and a whole bunch of delightful salads from Martha (http://www.esva.net/martha/salads.htm). Harry (http://www.hfm.com/rec_soup.html) has his favorite soups, such as Turkey Tortilla, as does Chef Rick Kangas with his Watermelon Gazpacho (http://foodstuff.com/pearl/rec-sou.html).

SAUCES

Sauces are sometimes a stumbling block for beginning cooks. Even the pros can have their problems with a béarnaise sauce that turns to (rich and delicious but) scrambled eggs in the blink of an eye.

You can start with a nice collection of some traditional (ketchup) and some less traditional (Chow Chow) sauces at http://www.culinaria.com/collectedRecipes/sauces.html from Michael Aichlmary.

Even if you can find a specific sauce using one of the search engines mentioned earlier, at least visit the Dinner's Coop sauce list (http://dinnercoop.cs.cmu.edu/cgi-bin/aglimpse/01/Recipes?query=sauce&whole=on&errors=0&maxfiles=100&maxlines=Interent E-mail),

RECIPE: ORANGE-SOY MARINADE FOR CHICKEN OR VEAL (4 SERVINGS)

This marinade lends a delicious flavor to chicken, Cornish hens and veal chops. Good side dishes are spiral pasta or steamed rice, along with sugar snap peas or green beans. Orange slices and green onions make a fresh, pretty garnish.

¼ cup soy sauce
¼ cup strained orange juice
2 tbsp strained lemon juice
1 tbsp oil
1 tbsp honey
1 tsp grated orange zest
½ tsp grated lemon zest
1 medium shallot, minced
1 tsp ground ginger
¼ tsp ground cloves
Dash black pepper
4 chicken breast halves with skin and bones, or
4 medium veal chops

Mix together soy sauce, orange and lemon juices, oil, honey, orange and lemon zest, shallot, ginger, cloves, and pepper in shallow dish. Add chicken. Cover and refrigerate, turning regularly, until needed. Grill meat as desired. Marinade can be reserved, brought to boil in small saucepan, and served as light sauce for grilled meat.

where you'll find recipes for Mark's Red Chile Sauce, Raspberry Sauce (for chocolate cake), Pesto, and Beef Marinade. Because this page is full of links to the actual recipes for these sauces, use the Find option on your browsers to locate references to what you want to cook.

SEAFOOD

Now that you can get fresh seafood at almost any grocery store in the United States, there's more opportunity to cook and enjoy it. The Internet Channel Index (http://fiddle.ee.vt.edu/proto/ Entertainment/Food_and_Eating/Recipes/Seafood/) leads off with three excellent links to seafood recipes including the *Alaska Seafood Cookbook* (http://www.state.ak.us/local/akpages/

COMMERCE/asmihp.htm), brought to you by the State of Alaska and the State of Alaska Marketing Institute; Creelers Recipe of the Week (http://www.demon.co.uk/creelers/recipe.html), which the week I looked was Filetti di Pesce Oreganato; the Hawaii Seafood Buyers Guide (http://planet-hawaii.com/hsbg/); Little Dave's Recipe of the Week (http://www.lainet.com/~eatfish/recipe.htm), which the week I looked was Baked Stuffed Lobster; and a link to the Seafood Recipe Archives (http://www.cs.cmu.edu/~mjw/recipes/seafood/seafood.html), with recipes for Paella, Dad's Mussels, Seafood Pot Pie, and Stuffed Squid.

The Alaska Seafood Marketing Institute home page also contains links for suppliers, industry literature, and related links, and a download area for more information about fish recipes, fish in general, and the state's efforts to preserve this billion dollar industry.

Finally, Sainsbury's, a United Kingdom supermarket conglomerate, offers a nice selection of a little bit out of the ordinary seafood recipes such as Poached Salmon with Mushrooms and Leeks; Apricot, Pistachio, and Coriander Stuffed Trout; and Creamy Plaice at http://www.j-sainsbury.co.uk/recipes/seafood.html.

VEGETARIAN

If you thought that nuts and berries were the main staples of the vegetarian's diet, take another look. In the last 10 years, the vegetarian craze has entered the main market and has become one of the most rapidly growing food areas. Why? Because many health conscious cooks people are finding it to be an attractive alternative.

One of the best starting points is Great Vegetarian Recipes (http://members.aol.com/meadowscd/recipes/index.html), featuring Chinese, American, Dessert, and Bread dishes from Debbie Meadows. A nice added feature of Debbie's home page is that you can sign her guest book, then view the records of others who have signed in and pick up even more information about vegetarian cooking. Then point your browsers at Vegetarian Pages (http://www.veg.org/veg/), where you'll not only find loads of recipes, but also information about being a vegetarian, major events, books and software, and even bios of famous vegetarians such as Kim Basinger (actress), Albert Einstein (scientist), Billy Idol (rock star), and supermodel Christy Brinkley.

Three other good vegetarian sites are The Vegetarian Society (`http://www.veg.org/veg/Orgs/VegSocUK/info.html`), The Low-Fat Vegetarian Archive (`http://www.fatfree.com/`), and Veggie Heaven (`http://www.webserve.co.uk/Veggie/`), where you can find nutritional information and a question and answer section.

The Low Fat Vegetarian site contains a fat-free searchable recipe index with over 2,900 recipes organized into 50 categories including soups, desserts, and Indian food. A search for garbanzo beans (chick-peas) yielded recipes for hummus, chili, and pasta salads.

If you can't find any vegetarian recipe that works for the pot luck, send them a greeting card with a vegetarian recipe inside from Gourmet Greetings at `http://mendez5000.com/gourmetgreetings/`.

TIP

When you use any search engine and click on the first URL listed, be sure to explore that home page for other links that may be even more relevant to what you are looking for. The first link shown may be the most apparently related to your search words, but it may not have the most of what you need.

◄ BEER ►

Beer on America Online
•
Beer on Compuserve
•
Beer on Microsoft Network
•
General Beer Pages
•
Virtual Pub and Beer Emporium
•
Drink Your Own
•
Cooking with Beer
•
Clubs and Organizations
•
For Collectors Only
•
Your Local Beer Guide
•
Personal Beer Pages

There are more than 300 manufacturers of beer, millions of barrels of beer are produced and consumed each year, and this is the first year that the price has gone up in 5 years. Where did we get all this information? The Beer Institute, of course, at `http://www.beerinst.org/inst/fun/cook.htm`. With all that beer being consumed, it's no surprise that there are thousands of good places online to learn about beer, from making it to drinking it to ordering it through a beer of the month club.

BEER ON AMERICA ONLINE

The best place to start on America Online if you're interested in beer is the Food and Drink Network (keyword: *Beer*). Among other beer-related resources, you'll find Beer & Beer Brewing Message Boards, information about *Beer* Magazine, Beer Columnists & Articles (only one article in this category when we checked), and a collection of files contributed by members about homebrewing, coaster trading, and beer supplies.

As with many America Online forums, this one is sponsored by several different companies, among them the Bloomington Brewing Company (`http://bbc.bloomington.com`), a microbrewery in Bloomington, Indiana. Thinking about starting your own microbrewery? Take a look at Bloomington's business plan.

BEER ON COMPUSERVE

CompuServe finds us visiting the Bacchus Wine & Beer forum, where you'll find forums about beer that can take you from brewing to tasting to buying.

Beers & Breweries contains news, directories, calendars of events, lists, tasting notes, and other information about commercial breweries, microbreweries, and brewpubs in the United States and Canada and around the world.

Beer Tasting Notes is a collection of tasting notes from members about commercial beers.

General Homebrewing can provide you with all the information you need to brew your own, be you a novice or an expert. Among the topics you'll find here are discussions of brewing techniques, sanitation, fermentation, and bottling.

Technical Homebrew contains information about more advanced brewing topics such as yeast function and reproduction, grain use in both extract and full-grain beers, and hop utilization.

Need equipment? The Homebrew Equipment section contains information about the equipment used in brewing beer at home. You'll find information on just about everything you want and need to know to be successful.

Beer Recipes/Styles is where readers come together and offer what they've cooked up.

In the Clubs section, you'll find materials pertaining to the AHA (American Homebrewers Association), its publication (Zymurgy), and homebrew clubs and competitions (rules, results, schedules). For membership in AHA, write PO Box 1510, Boulder, CO 80306; call (303) 447-0816; fax (303) 447-2825; or send a message to the AHA's James Spence at UserID 70740.1107@compuserve.com.

Another outstanding resource on CompuServe is The Good Pub Guide. Here you can search for a pub, get a recommendation, or browse through the database of pubs. Stuck on the road and looking for a good pub? Get out the notebook computer, dial into CompuServe, and then search by county, town, pub name, and the number of stars it has received.

BEER ON THE MICROSOFT NETWORK

The Find option on the Microsoft Network provides 115 bulletin boards, files to download, folders, and more that contain at least some information about beer, but the hot spot is the Wine, Beer, Spirits & Cigars subforum shown on the next page. Here you'll find a spirited discussion on the hottest coasters, beer in London, Bells Amber beer, and just about anything else related to beer you can think of. It's a bit of a disorganized free-for-all, but the treat is in browsing through the various threads and conversations and learning more about beer than you thought existed.

You certainly don't want to ignore the various types of beers that have folders of their own, including white beer, black beer, classic beer, beer of the seasons, rye beer, and Trappist beer. Just double-click on any one and join the conversation.

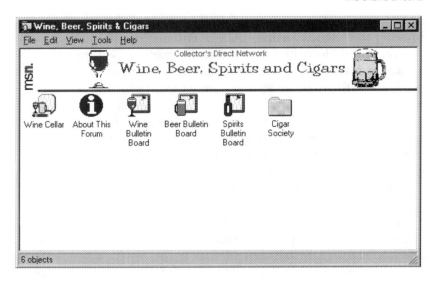

GENERAL BEER PAGES

As usual, the best place to start is with the giant pages that refer you to all kinds of other places such as the Beer & Brewing Index (`http://www.beerinfo.com/~jlock/wwwbeer.html`), which contains beer sites, breweries, brewpubs, and related resources; commercial beer listings; regional beer guides; beer festivals; and beer-related software.

Through the Beer Info Source (`http://www.beerinfo.com/~jlock/beerinf3.html`) you can connect with freelance beer writers Stan Hieronymus and Daria Labinsky, get started brewing your own with The MadBrewers, and visit Spencer's Beer Page (perhaps the first one of its kind on the Web).

If you're still looking to get started, try breWorld at `http://www.breworld.com/`, which has an attractive home page as you can see on the opposite page. Here you can connect to many other beer sites, look for a job in the brewing industry, or post a notice you're looking for one and get a good start in homebrewing. You can even get instructions on how to participate in tasting online.

[WHAT'S NEW] [BREWERS] [NEWS] [EDITOR'S PAGE] [breWORLD] [PUBLICATIONS] [EVENTS] [ORGANISATIONS]

Welcome to breWorld - the biggest beer & brewing Internet Site in Europe.

Erstes Internet-Seminar für die Brau - und Getränkeindustrie 16/17.10 Bamberg

---

- *Welcome to breWorld* -

NEW *Visit the breWorld Pubs page.*

Have you looked at our large and extensive homebrewing area.

Please help us to improve our site by answering a few questions about how you use us and what you would like to see - we are not asking you for your details.

- See the **breWorld** general index, or use our new search facility.
- Leave your comments and suggestions about **breWorld** for all to see in our guestbook.
- Which breweries are on **breWorld**?
- Find out how to book a Beer Tasting on-line.

....

[Search]   [Help]

We'll end with the Good and Bad of Beers (`http://www.ftech.net/~doom/beer2.html`), and we'll let the list of links to other sites speak for itself. Here's just a small sample from the beginning of the list.

alt.beer	Beer Recipes Using Extracts
American Homebrewers Association	Beer Hunter
Austrian Beer Guide	Beer InfoNet
Beer Games	Beer and Adventure
Beer Classified Ads	Beer and Homebrewing
Beer Survey	Brewery
Brew Your Own	Real Beer Page

VIRTUAL PUB & BEER EMPORIUM

If you are interested in brewing your own beer, start with the largest virtual homebrewing club in the word—HomeBrew Digest (`http://dezines.com/@your.service/cbm/digest.html`). This is a mailing list, and when you subscribe, you'll receive a daily flow of questions and answers to homebrewing questions. To signup, send e-mail to `majordomo@aob.org`. In your message type "subscribe homebrew-digest" in the body.

Now that you're in the loop and receiving information, visit Basement Brewin' (`http://www.coffey.com/~brewshop/BBHome.html`), which offers basics about brewing as well as supplies and kits for the novice brewmeister; Beer at Home (`http://www.beerathome.com/~beer/`), where Andy Causey acts as your personal instructor and sells supplies at this comprehensive site; and The Brewery (`http://alpha.rollanet.org/`), which includes a library of technical articles, recipes (for making beer not for cooking with beer), a listing of online resources, and the Tap Room, where you can read other people's tasting notes.

Don't ignore an excerpt from *50 Great Homebrewing Tips* (3rd Edition) by David Weisberg (`http://mgfx.com/homebrew/hb50tips/index.htm`), a nice collection of things you should and shouldn't do.

After you've read about brewing at home and even attended a club meeting in your area, it may be time to shop for supplies.

You can find virtually everything you need to brew online, and suppliers are all over the Web. The Beer Classifieds—Brewing Supplies (http://www.beerinfo.com/~jlock/beerads1.html) lists over 30 pages of companies located in all over the United States and Canada that carry everything from bottles to barrels to beakers. If you can't find it here, then you can't find it. Almost every entry has an e-mail or home page URL associated with it, or you can virtually shop around to find out who has exactly what you need and cost compare as well.

There are even brew your own facilities such as BYOB (Be Your Own Brewmaster) (http://www.byob.com/), where you actually brew your own beer, and U Brew Seattle (http://www.poppyware. com/ubrew/). U Brew Seattle is an especially informative home page answering questions such as how long it will take (about 2 hours to brew and, 2 weeks later, an hour to bottle) and how much it will cost (Crystal Cream Ale is $75 for 9 gallons for example). Visits to such places sound like great fun.

DRINK YOUR OWN

These can be fun, either as a present to yourself or to a beer-loving friend. Imagine having delivered each month to your door a sample of the country's most interesting beer from microbreweries far and wide. If you decide to join any one of these clubs, be sure to read the membership agreement very carefully and note that there are certain states that clubs are not allowed to deliver to.

There are at least 13 different clubs, such as 800-Microbrew (http://www.800-microbrew.com/). For $24.99, you get 12 bottles delivered, consisting of pilsners, ales, and stouts, such as Holiday Salute, Atlantic Amber, White Cloud Ale, and Three Finger Jack—their names are as distinctive as their taste. The Great American Beer Club (http://www.greatclubs.com/beerclub.html) or 1-800-Try-A-Sip ;-), delivers three 4-packs plus a newsletter for $15.95. They also offer basic kits for homebrewing, beer stuff (t-shirts, etc.), and recipes for cooking with beer.

RECIPE: SOUTHERN-STYLE FRIED CHICKEN BREASTS WITH BEER GRAVY
(from The Great American Beer Club)

The entire family loves chicken, and Southern-style with gravy is best!
Recommended beer: Amber lager or pale ale.

½ cup flour
½ tsp pepper
½ tsp salt
6 boneless chicken breasts
3 tbsp vegetable oil

Gravy
2 tbsp reserved seasoned flour
1 cup milk
¾ cup beer
⅛ cup water

Combine flour, pepper, and salt in a plastic bag. Add chicken, one piece at a time, and shake the bag to coat thoroughly. Reserve unused flour. Heat oil in a large, heavy skillet over medium heat and fry the chicken until crispy and golden brown on all sides. Remove chicken and drain on paper towels. Add the reserved flour to the pan drippings and stir until smooth. Gradually add milk, then beer, stirring constantly until the gravy is smooth and thick. Adjust the consistency with the water, if necessary. Arrange the chicken on a warm serving platter and ladle the gravy over the top. Garnish with fresh parsley and toasted, slivered almonds, if desired.

If you want pizza with your beer, try the (here it comes) Gourmet Pizza Club (http://www.greatclubs.com/pizzaclub.html), where you can get three 12-inch pizzas for $25.95. Remember 1-800-Try-A-Sip? How about 1-800-Mama-mia!

If either of these clubs don't do it, try World Beer Direct (http://www.worldbeerdirect.com/), where you can join one of five different beer of the month clubs.

COOKING WITH BEER

Beer is a terrific ingredient to cook with for several reasons. It adds a rich, full-bodied flavor and can be found in recipes for everything from soups to dips. It's great for use as a baking liquid because its carbonation adds a lightness and buoyancy to biscuits, pancakes, and cakes.

TIP: HOW COLD SHOULD BEER BE?
(from the Beer Institute's Favorite Recipes with Beer home page)

Experience shows that most people prefer drinking beer which is chilled to about 40 to 42 degrees Fahrenheit (4 to 6 degrees Celsius). This is when beer tastes most delicious. It's a temperature best obtained by storing beer on the bottom shelf of the refrigerator, away from the freezing section. Once removed from the refrigerator, beer should be served before it warms up. For a large party, beer may be chilled in any large container. Let the ice melt and add cold water. Check water temperature with a thermometer, if available. Just keep your beer cans or bottles in this cold water.

The Beer Institute has a great Cooking with Beer (http://www.beerinst.org/inst/fun/cook.htm) home page that includes recipes for salads, entrees, vegetables, breads, basting sauces, desserts, and late suppers, and tips on storing, serving, and pouring beer.

You'll also find recipes devoted to people who like good food and good beer at the Cooking with Beer home page (http://www.dra.nl/~rubbeer/cookbook/index.html), which was under construction when we visited.

CLUBS AND ORGANIZATIONS

Just as there are clubs and organizations for computer and car enthusiasts, you'll find the same for the beer crowd at http://www.beerinfo.com/~jlock/beerads5.html. The mother of all beer organizations is the Beer Institute (http://www.beerinst.org/), the official trade association, which represents over 220 members. This is the political side of things. The more fun side of things begins with the American Homebrewers Association (http://www.aob.org/aob/aob.html#AHA), which consists of 23,000 members and provides support and advice on the art and science of homebrewed beer. When you join, you get the quarterly magazine Zymurgy. The parent organization is the Association of Brewers (http://www.aob.org/aob/aob.html), a not-for-profit organization devoted to the collection and dissemination of beer and brewing information. Along with the American Homebrewers Association, the Association of Brewers includes the Institute for Brewing Studies (http://www.aob.org/aob/contents.html#IBS),

Brewers Publications (http://www.aob.org/aob/bp/bp.html), and the Great American Beer Festival (http://www.aob.org/aob/gabf/gabf. html). The festival is the largest American beer festival, and if you like beer, it's the place to be. In 1996, this get-together of 25,000 beer lovers was witness to over 1,400 different beers. Even if you're not a beer drinker, the nonalcoholic and food events make it a must-do. See the home page for directions and schedules.

Don't ignore your local club. Most stores that sell beer brewing supplies are connected with the people in town who brew and can probably give you information about local clubs. You can find home pages and information about local clubs in such places as Atlanta, Birmingham, Staten Island, New York, and Puget Sound through the http://www.beerinfo.com/~jlock/ beerads5.html home page , or how about the Mystiqu Krew of Brew Club (at http://www.neosoft.com/~dosequis/homepage.html) serving St. Tamany Parish in Louisiana or the Crazy Homebrewers club (http://www.netins.net/showcase/spsbeer/crazy/)?

FOR COLLECTORS ONLY

There's probably nothing that isn't collected, and beer can lovers (and collectors)will find home pages galore, including Mike Laere's Can Collection, which features over 1,600 different cans. DeJean's Beer Page (http://imol.vub.ac.be/~jqdoumen/ ElJuanElIncredibile.html) is a personal page about beer in general, including a (very long) listing of international beer labels (mostly from Belgium) and International beer cans and beer bottle caps. One of the things that's really appealing about this home page is that the labels in DeJean's collection have been scanned and are available for viewing.

If you're interested in collecting beer steins, then there's Stein Collectors International, Inc. (http://paterson.k12.nj. us/~steins/), founded in 1965, with a worldwide membership of over 2,000 collectors. These people know just about everything there is to know about beer steins, and there's a bulletin board full of questions and answers to prove it. You can also find out more about the organization, join, read an introduction to the collecting hobby, and learn about the annual convention, where they probably give as favors (what else?) beer steins.

YOUR LOCAL BEER GUIDE

Finally, there's the host of local guides to beer, one of the best organized of which is The New York City Beer Guide (http://www.nycbeer.org/index.html), which starts by telling you how the 77 breweries in New York City in 1890 had slipped just a few years ago to just one or two, and The World Wide Web of Beer (http://www.nycbeer.org/links/). The good news is that microbreweries have come back strong all over America. This home page tells you where beer is brewed (http://www.nycbeer.org/brewpubs.html) and where you can taste it (http://www.nycbeer.org/drinking.html), buy it at stores that have a great selection (http://www.nycbeer.org/stores.html), and learn more about it through literature, beer clubs, mailing lists, and tours.

PERSONAL BEER PAGES

Finally, there are the hundreds of personal beer pages covering just about everything that people have contributed to the Web. Yahoo! lists more than 60 at http://www.yahoo.com/Entertainment/Drinks_and_Drinking/Alcoholic_Drinks/Beer/Personal_Beer_Pages/, including the (hilarious) Bad Beer of the Month (http://207.43.106.35:80/badbeer/); the Beer Cap Collection (http://www.primenet.com/~jrblutt/beercap.html); Bajas Tour '96 (http://home.sn.no/~gwalther/bajas.htm), "the holiday where men are men, and everything is forgotten the next day"; The Fat Boy Funhouse (http://www.geocities.com/SunsetStrip/3327/); and Robert's ("In heaven there might be one beer. That's why we drink it here.") Ultimate Beer Page (http://www.caiw.nl/~rbgoudsw/index.html).

If you like the Blues along with your beer, try Jim's Blues 'N' Brews at http://www.cloud9.net/~leftwich/.

◄ CHEESE ►

Cheese on America Online

•

Cheese on Compuserve

•

Cheese on Microsoft Network

•

General Cheese Pages

Sometimes when you're hunting for particular information on the Internet about a food such as cheese, you just don't quite know what you'll find. Lots of people eat and enjoy it, but during our exploring, even the search engines (at first) didn't come up with much. It wasn't until about the fourth or fifth page of Web site listings that we hit gold. Here's the result of the work: a diverse, entertaining (be sure to check out Dr. Cheese), and comprehensive set of resources about perhaps the simplest of all foods.

CHEESE ON AMERICA ONLINE

If you want recipes and discussion about cheese, go to the Vegetarian (keyword: *vegan*) area on America Online. In the Vegetarian Dialogue and Vegetarian Library areas, you can find discussions and recipes about cheese and its uses.

CHEESE ON COMPUSERVE

The only cheese-related information on CompuServe is located in sites that sell cheese, and we'll cover those in the chapter "Shopping Online."

CHEESE ON THE MICROSOFT NETWORK

The Microsoft Network gave us a Dairy Cattle Discussion and Marty and the Trouble with Cheese when we used the Find option, so we'll pass on these.

GENERAL CHEESE PAGES

CHEESENET (http://www.wgx.com/cheesenet/)

CheeseNet is an attractive Web site organized by Kyle Whelliston that is packed with information and may be the first and last stop you have to make if you want to know what cheese is, how to make it, and where else you can go on the Internet to find out about it.

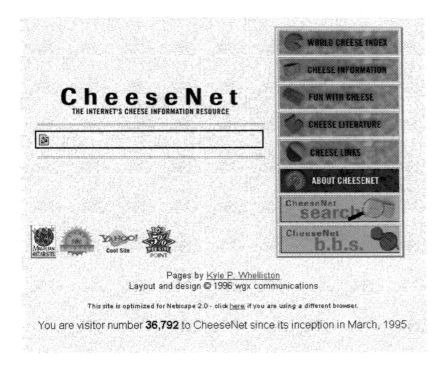

CheeseNet begins with The World Cheese Index (http://www.wgx.com/cheesenet/wci/), a database of over 60 cheeses including pictures of each cheese and information about each. You search by the first letter in the name (C for Camembert, S for Stilton, etc.) and you get back a picture and a nice description, as you can see here. You can also search for, and learn about, cheeses by their country of origin such as Fyno from Denmark, Feta from Greece, and Tallegio from Italy.

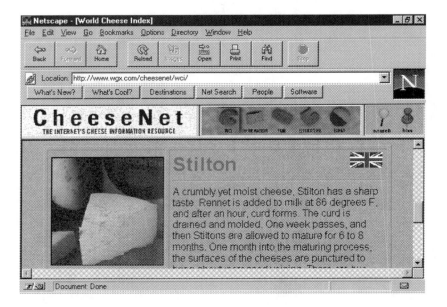

Cheese Information (http://www.wgx.com/cheesenet/info/) is a tutorial on the history of cheese (a gift to us from the Middle East), basic cheesemaking (fresh milk and only clean containers!), types of cheese (you name it and it's described here), and a cheese glossary. You probably know what the holes are in Swiss cheese, but what about persille? (It's a French term for a blue-veined cheese.)

Fun with Cheese (http://www.wgx.com/cheesenet/fun/) was under construction when we visited, but plans are for it to be a site where games, puzzles, and trivia contests will be offered.

You might not think of anything romantic or funny to say about cheese, but the Cheese Literature home page (`http://www.wgx.com/cheesenet/lit/`) in CheeseNet offers plenty. Want some Muenster Musings? An untitled poem? How about a story titled Cheese Grating Time? All here and more.

Finally, Cheese Links (`http://www.wgx.com/cheesenet/links/`) provides a long list of links to other cheese-related sites, some of which we will explore later in this section. You'll find links to basic information about making cheese and cheese recipes (some great links here), vendors, newsgroups, and a miscellaneous category.

CHEESE!

(`http://www.crayola.cse.psu.edu:80/~jrichard/cheese/ cheese.html`)

Here's the second valuable cheese page that connects you to many other resources. If you haven't had your fill of cheese after visiting CheeseNet, point your browser to Cheese!, which contains a list of links to other cheese related sites such as Mr. Cheese's World of Cheese! (`http://www.princeton.edu/~gprudhom/ cheese/`) including pointers to more cheese pages (including Houses of Cheese Worship!) and more cheese history; Global Cheese Online (`http://ccwf.cc.utexas.edu/~hope/global.html`), which includes the It's Better Than Cheez Whiz, It's Cheeze Quiz (`http://ccwf.cc.utexas.edu/~hope/chezquiz.html`) and The Cheese Page (`http://www.zennet.com/cheese/`) for those who need help identifying (by picture) rare cheeses. By the way, The Cheese Page won an Excellence in Oddity award and if you visit, you'll see why.

POEM FROM CHEESENET LITERATURE
(`http://www.wgx.com/ cheesenet/lit/`)

Cheese Haiku
by Leonard Weller

Cheese like a river
   flowing
Down asparagus
My heart leaps with
   gratitude

QUESTIONS FROM THE CHEEZ QUIZ (`http://ccwf.cc.utexas.edu/~hope/chezquiz.html`)

Where can you find basil leaf, horseradish, and blue cheese ice cream?
a. Canada
b. France
c. Japan
d. Graceland

What European game, similar to bowling, involves rolling or throwing a thick, flat, wooden "cheese" down an alley?
a. Cheese Rolling
b. Boules
c. Jurling
d. Skittles

MAKE YOUR OWN

The New England Cheesemaking Supply Company (http://www.cheesemaking.com/) shows up on just about every home page having anything to do with cheese. In business since 1976, they sing the praises of fresh, homemade cheese and provide an extensive Web site with lots of links to everything about making cheese from the basics to cheesemaking as a hobby, recipes, and more.

According to this cheesemaking company, making cheese at home is much easier than most people imagine, and they can get you started inexpensively through such starting kits as the Mozzarella kit for $19.95. It comes with the Mozzarella cheese starter, cheese rennet tablets, a dairy thermometer, citric acid pH paper, and a recipe. Should you want a preview of the instruction for how to make cheese at home, try the Cheesemaking 101 link (http://www.cheesemaking.com/intro/cheez101.htm), which gives you a sense of how long it takes to make different types of cheese as well as how many different steps are involved. (This depends upon the type of cheese as well.) Should you be in the vicinity of New England Supply in Ashfield, Massachusetts, you can sign up for a hands-on workshop. Be sure to sign up early: Many workshops sell out fast. What fun that must be.

SOME CHEESE TERMS

Butterfat—The fat portion (cream) in milk. Butterfat can vary from 2.5 to 5.5% of the total weight of milk.

Cheese Starter Culture—A bacterial culture added to milk as the first step in making many cheeses. The bacteria produce an acid during their life cycle in the milk. There are two categories of starter culture: mesophilic and thermophilic.

Pressing—A step in cheesemaking during which the curds are placed in a cheesecloth-lined mold and placed under pressure to remove more whey.

White Mold—A white mold (Penicillium candidum) that is encouraged to grow on a number of soft cheeses in order to develop a pungent flavor. Camembert is perhaps the most famous of these.

RECIPES

These aren't the recipes for making cheese, although those are easily available on the Internet at `http://www.cheesemaking.com/recipes/`. These are recipes that use cheese as an ingredient.

For example, Cheese Recipes (`http://www.cs.cmu.edu/~mjw/recipes/cheese/index.html`) includes such delicious-sounding dishes as Brie en Croute, Cheese Soufflé, Fondue Vaudoise, and Cheese-Garlic biscuits (like the kind that are served at Red Lobster). In addition, there's a link to soup recipes that use cheese.

Then there's the host of individual recipes available as part of someone's home page or just sort of floating out there in cyberspace. You can try Cheese Blintzes (`http://ecep1.usl.edu/cajun/ent/10208.htm`), Artichoke Cheese Strata (`http://www.mal.com/~squealer/links/recipe.html`), and the most famous comfort food of all, macaroni and cheese, at several sites including `http://www.lib.uchicago.edu/keith/cookbook/recipes/macaroni-and-cheese.html` and `http://www.kuow.washington.edu/wkdy/recipes/r27.htm`. Don't dismiss the less traditional Nacho Style Macaroni and Cheese (`http://www.eat.com/cookbook/light/lt-nacho-macaroni-cheese.html`). Finally, the Columbus' Quincentennial (why it's named this is not clear) macaroni and cheese is at `http://www.ilovepasta.org/recipes/meatless/505.html`.

GOT A QUESTION?

Have a question about cheese? Ask Dr. Cheese at `http://www.wgx.com/cheesenet/info/drcheese.html`, where Dr. Emory K. Cheese will actually answer your cheese-related question. Then, if you have questions about what kind of wine to serve with what cheese, try the Cheese & Wine Matching Page at `http://www.sumacridge.com/wineconn/cheese.htm`. Here you'll find lists of cheeses and the wines that are recommended to go with them.

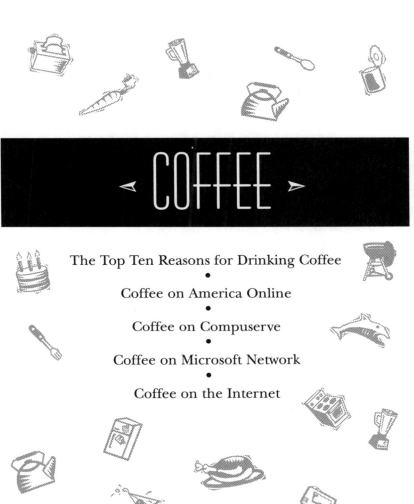

◄ COFFEE ►

If you go to Coffee a GoGo (`http://www.illuminatus.com/fun/agogo/coffee_a_gogo.html`), you'll find these top ten reasons for drinking coffee, and if you go just about anywhere else online that has to do with food, you'll find something about coffee as well, usually about buying it.

THE TOP TEN REASONS FOR DRINKING COFFEE

10. It's good to the last drop.
 9. I'm a mover and a shaker.
 8. All my friends do it.
 7. It looks cool.
 6. Yellow teeth are sexy.
 5. Don't touch my hand when I reach for my coffee!
 4. It's an addiction.
 3. I can quit any time. I drink it for the flavor.
 2. If it ain't broke, don't fix it.
 1. It's a get-rich-quick scheme, spill it in your lap, like an idiot, and sue McDonalds.

Enough humor for now. Let's turn to the major online services and see how they can help the coffee gourmet.

COFFEE ON AMERICA ONLINE

Although Café Starbucks is a commercial site, it has lots of useful information for the coffee buff, including tips on brewing good coffee at home, a worldwide tasting guide, and their monthly newsletter. You won't be surprised to learn that you can order coffee from them here as well.

TIPS : HOW TO MAKE PERFECT COFFEE (FROM THE PEOPLE AT STARBUCKS ON AOL)

The starting point for making great coffee is to think of it as a form of cooking. To be successful, you need to follow a proven recipe and use the best ingredients you can. This is fairly easy to do, and we have attempted to make it simple by formulating the "Four Fundamentals." Understand and follow each of them, and you're on your way to brewing a great cup of coffee every time.

1. **Proportion:** Use the right proportion of coffee to water. This is the most important step in making great coffee. Brewing coffee is the process of using hot water to extract desirable flavor components and mix them with water. Too much water or too little coffee results in overextracted and bitter coffee. If the resulting brew is too strong for your taste, simply dilute it with hot water after brewing rather than using less coffee.

2. **Grind:** How finely or coarsely your coffee is ground determines how quickly water will pass through it, and thus the nature of the flavor elements that end up in your coffee. Many different brewing methods exist, and each one has a particular grind requirement.
   While it may be tempting to grind finer in an attempt to use less coffee, the result is bitter, overextracted coffee: the finer grind slows the water down too much. Conversely, a grind that is too coarse produces coffee that's weak and underextracted. If you grind your own coffee, we recommend you grind your beans fresh each time. As the size of correct grind differs with varying coffeemakers, please use the grinding information that follows for your specific brewing method.
   - Plunger Pot/Percolator Grind: Approximately 6 seconds in a blade grinder.
   - Drip Grind: Approximately 10 seconds in a blade grinder.
   - Cone Filter Grind: Approximately 25 seconds in a blade grinder.
   - Espresso Grind: Best achieved by using a burr grinder.

3. **Water:** Use fresh, cold water. A cup of coffee is 98% water. So the water you use to make coffee should taste clean, fresh, and free of impurities. Avoid water from a water softener, water that tastes like chlorine, or water that tastes or smells like iron or sulfur. If your tap water tastes good to drink, it's likely to make good coffee. Water just off the boil (195 to 205 degrees F) is just right for extracting the coffee's full range of flavors. Any cooler and it can't adequately do the job. Automatic coffee makers heat the water for you; make sure the one you use gets the water hot enough. If you use a kettle to heat water, remove it from the heat for a few seconds after boiling, and then pour.

4. **Freshness:** Start with freshly roasted beans, freshly ground, and drink the coffee freshly brewed. Coffee's enemies are oxygen and moisture. To keep coffee for more than two weeks, store it in the freezer in the smallest practical airtight container. For the best results, grind your coffee fresh each time you make it. Whole bean coffee stays fresh longer because less of its surface is exposed to oxygen. By grinding beans each time, you preserve the coffee's freshness.

   Brewed coffee is best held in a thermal carafe. Don't leave coffee on a burner more than 20 minutes, and avoid reheating, as the result is a bitter-tasting brew.

COFFEE ON COMPUSERVE

We find ourselves starting at the Bacchus Wine & Beer forum and the Coffee & Tea area, where there are several topics including coffee-related publications, the merits of using gold filters, and even a recipe for barbecued pork butt marinated in coffee. You can also purchase coffee from Coffee Anyone.

COFFEE ON THE MICROSOFT NETWORK

The **Find** command on the Microsoft Network icon in the taskbar takes us to a fairly rich set of resources on coffee, beginning with the ICNN Coffee Break folder. As you can see here, there are some interesting messages including how to buy coffee, how to make the perfect cup, some java jargon (what's a winey or earthy cup of coffee?), and an entire other folder on espresso, a strong filtered (later produced under pressure) coffee based on Turkish coffee, but introduced by the Italians.

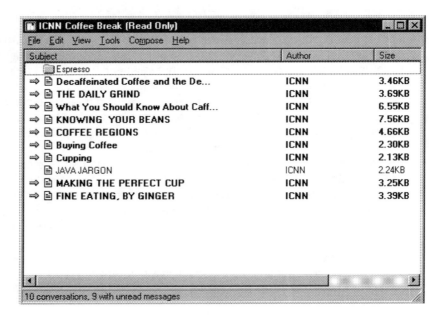

There are several chat rooms and probably America Online's best coffee resource—the Coffee Club Cyber Café, which offers The Koala Café, the Coffee Cappuccino Lounge, the Coffee Expresso Lounge, Coffee Rooms in which to talk with other coffee aficionados, and coffee recipes.

COFFEE ON THE INTERNET

The majority of coffee activity on the Internet lists coffeehouses and sites where you can purchase coffee, but there are some others that are interesting and fun as well.

GENERAL COFFEE PAGES

Coffee a GoGo (http://www.illuminatus.com/fun/agogo/coffee_a_gogo.html), shown on the next page, has everything from an offer for free coffee to a discussion of coffee history to an kind of URL roulette for coffee where you go to a new coffee site each time you click on the Percolator icon.

The current contest for the free coffee asks you to go to various coffee-related Web pages and find the dancing coffee bean, putting together the words that are associated with the beans. If you're right and your submission is selected (at random from all the correct ones), you win 2 pounds of Summit Coffee. The Perc-O-Matic on the Go-Go page takes you (at random) to a coffee-related site. We went to Why Coffee is Better Than Women (http://www.me.mtu.edu/~loew/coffee_women.html), the **Coffee Corner** (http://www.tue.nl/wtb/wpa/se/klerk/cofcorn.htm), **Coffee Lover's Heaven** (http://www.edu.yorku.ca/~tcs/~adawson/coffee.html), and **Coffee Links** (http://www-personal.engin.umich.edu/~cbrokaw/)—all lots of fun.

The second best coffee place is Coffeetopia (http://www.webventure.com/coffeetopia/index.cgi), a compendium of All About Coffee (some history), Upcoming Events, and a link to other intrusting coffee Web sites (mostly coffeehouses that offer Internet connections for patrons).

Open
24 hours

Welcome to Coffee a GoGo
We got lots brewing
So, park it where you please.

The Menu

FREE COFFEE!

Yeah that's right, I said free coffee!

The Buzz

A calm, unpretentious atmosphere
in which to discuss coffee.

Coffee Quest (http://www.inetcafe.com/bev/cq/coffhome.htm) offers *The Java Journal* (a newsletter), a featured flavor of the month (an interesting treatise on African coffees the month this site was explored), Coffee Archives (including the previous month's featured articles with titles such as "What Coffee Do You Serve with…?" and "Flavor Profiles"), Coffee forum (for exchanging ideas), and Club Membership (for joining the club where you get 2 pounds each month for $16.95).

INFORMATION ABOUT COFFEE

Some of the general pages mentioned earlier have information, but there are also pages devoted strictly to educating you about the world of coffee.

If you're not sure of the three qualities of acidity in coffee (acid, sour, and process acidity), try the Glossary of Coffee Terminology (http://www.lucidcafe.com/lucidcafe/glossary.html), an 18-page listing of important terms from the coffee world put together by the fine folks at Lucid Café (http://www.lucidcafe. com/lucidcafe/). This is very serious business, with important distinctions made between tainted and tangy as qualities of taste. Stop here first if you want to impress your local brewmeister.

You can find out about different coffees from every part of the word through Cyber Café's listing of Coffee by Country (http://www.bid.com/bid/coffeeworld/java.html). Just the partial list here shows you how comprehensive the collection of information is: China Coffee, Colombian Coffee, Jamaican Coffee, Kona Coffee, Tanzania Coffee, and Yunnan Coffee. You can also find information about coffees from other lands through Coffee by Country (http://www.lucidcafe.com/lucidcafe/bycountry.html), a collection of 11 pages brought to you by the Lucid Café folks mentioned earlier.

Then you have the ramblings, ideas, and idiosyncratic presentations by people with their own coffee pages, such as Coffee (http://ice.bae.uga.edu/dept/ugrads/lerch/coffee.html), and agricultural and production information (http://www.weather. net/roemerwx/publications/tradewinds/tw-jan-95/coffee.html).

COFFEE SHOPS

A COFFEE CONTEST FROM COFFEE A GOGO

(http://www.
illuminatus.com/fun
/agogo/free.html)

Want to have
some fun? Each
week, the Coffee a
GoGo people think up
a contest that involves
an animated coffee
bean, questions, and
just a good time. Visit
and maybe you'll
come home 2 pounds
heavier (with coffee,
that is).

Most of the pages on the Web are devoted to various coffee shops and cafes, all offering what looks like a nice selection of services including a full product line of coffee and related equipment. These range from cyber cafes where you can pay $40 for 10 hours of Internet time to pages that sell coffee in bulk. Here's a representative sample.

Two coffeehouse home pages can get you started on what's available. Buckhead Coffee Houses/Coffee bar (http://www.buckhead.org/entertai/coffee.html) lists the coffee establishments in the Atlanta area, and Coffee Shops and Desserts (http://www.abilene.com/dining/tablecloth/bakery.html) lists more than you want (such as TCBY Yogurt and Jack n' Jill Donuts), but also a nice collection (but no links) of coffee shops in the Abilene, Texas, area.

If you're buying coffee, try these order-from-home Web sites. The Coffee Warehouse (http://www-015.connix.com/coffee/index.html) waits until it gets your order and then roasts the beans, ensuring that they're as fresh as possible. You're welcome to visit their factory for a tour in Bloomfield, Connecticut, or order anywhere from a few ounces to 500 pounds online.

T.C. Peabody's Espresso and Coffee Bar (http://home.revealed.net/peabody/bulk.html) offers an extensive list of freshly roasted beans with titles such as Kona Extra Fancy ($19 per pound), Gourmet Espresso ($9.40 per pound) and Italian Roast ($10 per pound). You contact them via phone (they don't want credit cards on line because the Internet is not secure enough for those kind of transactions), and they'll call you back and take your order.

Finally, there's Baby's Place Coffee Bar (http://www.vacation3.com/babys.html) the southernmost coffee roasters in America, offering Baby's Havana Roast, Killer Joe, and Baby's Private Buzz. What a way to wake up.

◄ TEA ►

Tea on America Online
•
Tea on CompuServe
•
Tea on Microsoft Network
•
Tea on the Internet

66"All the tea in China" is an expression that's true to its word. There's a lot of tea in China because there are a lot of people in China as well as the rest of the world who drink it. In fact, tea is consumed by more people than any other beverage but water. It was first commercially grown in China in the 8th century, introduced in Europe during the 12th century, and thrown off ships in the famous Boston Tea Party rebellion in 1773.

TEA ON AMERICA ONLINE

There's no information about tea on America Online, either using the Find button or looking in the Food and Drink Center. If you use America Online and want to talk about tea, the best bet is to go to a forum where people are discussing beverages and start a discussion at that location.

TEA ON COMPUSERVE

A search through the Bacchus Wine & Beer (Go word: *wine*) library using *tea* as the keyword reveals a set of interesting and diverse resources, including recipes for Long Island Iced Tea, Tea Driver, a Q&A file about coffee and tea, a list of coffee and tea magazines, and a comprehensive directory of (mostly) tea and (some) coffee vendors, a few of which are listed here. You can find similar listings including recipes about tea in the Cook's forum (Go word: *cooks* and search with the keyword *tea*).

The addresses are often accompanied by a recommendation from a CompuServe contributor, so you can get some idea as to what the store might have, learn a bit about its (and the owner's) character, and more.

If you look farther in CompuServe, you'll find a few entries in the Hong Kong forum (Go word: *hongkong*) about tea. One of these, The Tea Ceremony in a Chinese Wedding, shows the variety and unexpected nature of online contributions. The message is a very nicely written response to another CompuServe user who is getting married and wanted to know about the traditional Chinese tea ceremony. In response to the user's question, another CompuServe user came through with a detailed description of exactly what happens as well as the meaningfulness of the ceremony.

Benchley Tea
RD#1 178-G
Highway 34 & Ridgewood Rd.
Wall Township, NJ 07719

Cambridge Coffee, Tea,
and Spice House
1765 Massachusetts Ave.
Cambridge, MA 02138

Celestial Seasonings
4600 Sleepytime Drive
Boulder, CO 80301

Daruma Foods
1290 Sixth Street
Berkeley, CA 94710

Flavor Cup (M.O.)
also known as: Schapira
Coffee & Tea Company
117 West 10th Street
New York, NY 10011

The House of Tea
720 S. 4 St.
Philadelphia, PA

Myers of Keswick
634 Hudson St.
(just south of 14 St.)
New York, NY

TEA ON MICROSOFT NETWORK

Perhaps by coincidence, one of the opening messages on the Microsoft Network on the day we checked was about a pewter tea set available from Gourmet Gift Net. Maybe Microsoft Network users are big tea drinkers?

More to the point, if you use the Find option to search for tea, you'll find 16 mentions including the Tea Rooms (all chat rooms). These chats cover just about everything you would want to know about tea and other topics such as tea pastries, high tea, leaves versus bags, and any other topic you think that tea users might be interested in.

TEA GENERAL PAGES

It's true that more tea is consumed than other drinks, including coffee, but that doesn't mean there is more information on the Internet than for coffee or other beverages. Tea has the drinkers, but not the popularity, as is reflected by the relative scarcity of general pages on the Net. However, there are some general pages about tea.

We can start with (what else?) the Tea Pages (`http://www.nitehawk.com/bnielsen/`), which lists categories with links to other pages including authors, books, caddies, clippers, countries, encyclopedias, history, frequently asked questions, magazines, newsgroups, and vendors in addition to a description of tea use and sales in Burma, Sweden, the United States, and several other countries. All this hard work on tea central was done by Kai Birger Nielson and includes descriptions of her 192 tea caddies!

Another page full of valuable resources, links, and information is Tea as in Terrific (`http://www.pt.hk-r.se/~di92jn/tea.html`), which contains a wonderful picture of Alice's tea party with the Mad Hatter and friends. You can also find a listing of other tea pages, vendors galore, related material, and how to use tea in cooking including special recipes.

Daisan, Inc. offers the Japanese Green Tea home page (`http://www.daisan.co.jp/cha2e.htm`) with information about the origin of Japanese tea and Japanese green tea and health.

INFORMATION ABOUT TEA

Here's where the volume of pages increases and shows the diversity of offerings as well. To begin with, "Come in and join the conversation" at `http://www.xroads.com/~pct/tea.html`, where the art of tea and conversation is being reborn. You read what's recommended and then make a contribution to the ongoing conversation. This is not a chat room, but a place to submit a brief comment on the nature and content of the discussion going on. Of course, you're expected to pour yourself a cup of tea.

Under certain circumstances there are few hours in life more agreeable than the hour dedicated to the ceremony known as afternoon tea.
—Henry James

Love and scandal are the best sweeteners of tea.
—from Tea in the Literature
(`http://kiwi.futuri.net/tea/teaquote.htm`)

I am glad I was not born before tea.
—Sydney Smith, from Tea as in Terrific
(`http://www.pt.hk-r.se/~di92jn/tea.html`)

CAFFEINE AND TEA (from http://eMall.Com/Republic/Caffeine.html)

1. The longer the tea leaves have fermented during manufacture, the greater their caffeine content. Green tea, which is unfermented, has one-third the caffeine per cup as black tea, which is fully fermented. Oolong is semi-fermented and has about half as much caffeine as black tea
2. The shorter the brewing time, the less caffeine ends up in the cup. A four-minute infusion of black tea will produce 40 to 100 milligrams of caffeine, a three-minute infusion only about 20 to 40 milligrams.
3. The smaller the leaf, the stronger the extraction of caffeine. Using comparable amounts and brewing times, a tea bag filled with cut leaf or "dust" will release nearly twice as much caffeine per cup as full-leaf tea.
4. Caffeine's primary effects last about 15 to 45 minutes, depending on an individual's sensitivity.
5. Scientific studies of caffeine to date have been contradictory. There is no conclusive evidence that caffeine causes or exacerbates any specific illness or medical condition.

Then there are the more scholarly pages containing information about tea such as a description of the dedication of a Japanese tea garden (http://www.belmont.gov/orgs/alumni/smoke_f95_centen_tea.html), descriptions of herbal teas (such as Indian Love Tea and Warrior's Brew) and how they relate to the Indian culture (http://www.iw.net/users/h/herbtea/select.htm), all about caffeine and tea (http://eMall.com/Republic/Tea.html), and a page that touts tea for your health and enjoyment (http://www.teaworld.com/tea/), especially the green and oolong teas.

BUYING TEA

Finally, there are the hundreds of sites where you can purchase almost any tea that is available. Some appear on the general home pages that we described earlier, but most large retailers have pages of their own. For example, the Word Wide Web Sites for Tea pages (http://bohr.physics.upenn.edu/~bush/tea_sites.html) list about 20 different dealers, most of which you can order online. Some links have descriptions accompanying them as well.

The really big buying page is offered by Todd & Holland Tea Merchants (http://www.branchmall.com/teas/teas.html), with over 14 pages of different teas and their descriptions, all priced per ¼ pound (see next page). The Todd & Holland Tea Tour takes you for a tour of tea around the word, delivering either ¼ or ⅛ pound per month to your home (or office). Although their tea is not inexpensive ($220 for the 6-month Ancient China & Formosa tour), very small quantities of tea are necessary to make a cup, so ¼ pound is likely to last a long time. In addition to tea, Todd & Holland offer filters, blends, decaffeinated teas, assams (a hearty tea from India), keemuns (from China), and many other types.

TODD & HOLLAND TEA MERCHANTS
The issue is not affording the best teas....the issue is finding them.

Menu
- About Todd & Holland
- Letter from Bill Todd
- Tea Samplers, Gift Packages, Tea Tours
- Black Blends, Flavoured teas, Decaffinated teas
- Black Teas
- Semi-Black, Green and White Teas
- Accessories
- Holiday Gift Catalog
- Frequently Asked Questions
- Ordering Information

TODD & HOLLAND, TEA MERCHANTS
7577 Lake Street, River Forest, Illinois 60305, U S A
Phone: 1-800-747-8327 Fax: 708-488-1246
E-Mail: Teaman@Tea-Merchant.chi.il.us
URL: http://www.Rare-Teas.com/teas/teas.html

Go to the Branch Mall

Other large tea dealers are the Tea Business (http://www.asiainfo.com/plaza/hallway/Tuhsu-tea/eng/tea.html), which features meetea, gunpowder, lungching, black, and jasmine teas, and the Tea Vendor List (http://www.zumacafe.com/douglas/tea_vendor.html), a listing of vendors arranged alphabetically, tea accessories, books, magazines, and even museums such as the British Teapots and Tea Drinking in Norfolk, England.

◄ WINE ►

Wine on America Online
•
Wine on Microsoft Network
•
CompuServe Wine offerings
•
Internet offerings

I f you enjoy a fine wine, then you've probably attended a formal or informal wine tasting, but how about one where you're tasting a Bordeaux in New York City, your wine-tasting colleague is tasting a Pinot Grigio in Los Angeles and you're conversing with each other, not over the phone, but over the Internet?

It happened this past summer in New York and Los Angeles, where tasters from Websine, an Internet broadcaster connected with Talley Vineyards, used both audio and media to taste and talk about the wines they were sampling. A special Web site (`http://talley.websine.com`) was created for the event, and oenophiles from around the globe were invited to participate as well in the tasting of wines from four different regions in California: Santa Ynez Valley, Santa Martia Valley, Arroyo Grande Valley, and Edna Valley.

You can learn about wine, vicariously taste wine, and get any question you might have about buying, drinking, and serving wine answered on the Internet. Here's how.

WINE ON AMERICA ONLINE

Wine & Dine Online (keyword: *fdn*), shown here, offers everything from syndicated columnists to a wine dictionary to commentaries on what wine to drink with what food.

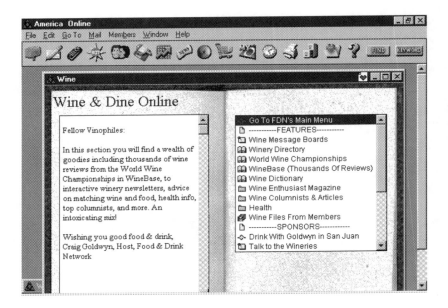

Start with WineBase to find out what the experts have to say about different types of wines. WineBase allows you to enter the type of wine and other characteristics that might describe what you would want your choice to be. For example, we entered Bordeaux and found 32 different wines reviewed, including this one for Mouton-Cadet 1990:

88-Mouton-Cadet 1990

SCORE (50-100):	88 (margin of error is + or - 3)
BRAND NAME:	Mouton-Cadet
VINTAGE:	1990
GRAPES COME FROM:	Bordeaux
WINERY IS IN:	France
WINE TYPE:	Red
CASES PRODUCED:	Production not disclosed
PRICE AT THE WINERY:	$8.99/750 ml
PRICE CATEGORY:	Inexpensive
REVIEWED BY:	The World Wine Championships
CONDUCTED BY:	The Beverage Testing Institute Inc.
DATE PUBLISHED:	11/93
AWARDS:	Silver Medal, National Champion

DESCRIPTION: For many years the quick-cash wine of the Chateau Mouton-Rothschild, it is now obviously much more. Made from purchased grapes and designed for quick and easy consumption, its light, bright red color hints at its light body. The nose is a melange of mint, eucalyptus, sage, and rye bread. It's imbued with simple, cola-tinged flavor and a youthful tannic finish. If red wine is heart-friendly, then party hearty with this French bargain.

Once you've gotten the information you want about a particular wine, you can go to one of the Wine Message Boards and talk with various wine mavens such as Jerry Mead or Phil Ward and inquire about the review or your selection, or even get a recommendation about another wine that you might want to sample. When it comes time to consider buying, either by the bottle or by the case, click on **Winery Directory** and you'll be able to find wineries that have the wine you want. The Winery Directory contains information on over 1,500 wineries in 43 states. In fact, America Online has tried to find every winery in the United States, so if you know of one that is not listed, e-mail them and they'll post it and be thankful for your assistance.

A quick search for champagne resulted in the wineries that produce a variety of different labels. Double-clicking on any one provides specific information such as the phone number and address.

Finish up with America Online and wine by visiting one of their sponsors, Wine Info Net. This commercial site has an extensive database of wineries, and you can review catalogs of wine and wine-related merchandise—and even look up the price of fine wines using the Wine Price File Online. If you like what you see, use America Online to make the purchase. You'll also find maps of vineyards and newsletters at this site, as well as reviews of wines and food, a library of articles and reviews from popular wine magazines, and newsletters that you can download, and you can join the Cellar Master Wine Club.

WINE ON THE MICROSOFT NETWORK

Use the **Find** feature in the Microsoft Network and you'll come up with around 125 places where you can go for information, including a wine guide bulletin board, how to save your money and buy good wines, discussions about wine cellars, an organic wine shop, and extensive discussions on health and wine.

We can start with the ICNN Food & Beverage Center forum, which contains the subforum Beverage Bazaar you see on the next page, containing links to the Beverage Bazaar bulletin board, Blue on Wine and More, and information about Paul Kreider's Winemaking School.

What's fabulous about the winemaking school is that you can attend from home. Paul puts together an informative, well-written, and entertaining column that appears each month in this subforum. For example, March 1996 contains a brief history of wine and what's needed to make about 5 gallons of wine at home. Although he uses wine expert's terminology, there is also a detailed glossary at the end of each lesson so you need not feel lost in a sea of new words. This is the kind of information and writing that makes you want to go out and buy all the equipment to make your own wines!

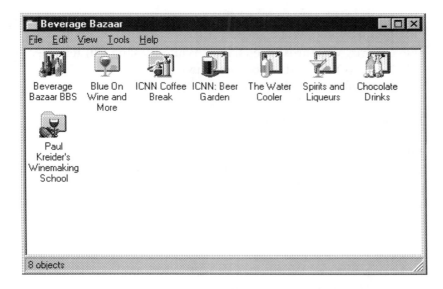

Another very useful subforum in ICNN Center is Blue on Wine and More. Anthony Dias Blue is a world-renowned wine authority and offers the Blue Library, book reviews, and a brief bio as well. The Wine Library lists 46 reviews of different wines. Here is a sample review of Mendocino wines:

It is interesting to note that no gold medals were awarded for 1993 zinfandel, 1992–3 cabernet, or petite sirah. With the exception of wines like the Obester zinfandel, these red varieties don't perform as well in the cool Mendocino conditions. If you are going to try some Mendocino wines, pinot noir, gewurztraminer, chardonnay, and sparklers are all good bets. You might start off with some of the gold medal winners from the Mendocino County Fair:

1994 Navarro Vineyards, Sauvignon Blanc
1992 Handley Cellars, Chardonnay, Anderson Valley
1993 Navarro Vineyards, Chardonnay, Premiere Reserve,
    Anderson Valley.
1994 Parducci Wine Cellars, Chardonnay
1994 Husch Vineyards, Chardonnay, La Ribera Vineyard
1994 Husch Vineyards, Chardonnay
1994 Navarro Vineyards, Gewurztraminer, Anderson Valley
1991 Handley Cellars, Brut Rose
1991 Scharffenberger Cellars, Blanc de Blancs

1994 Monte Volpe Pinot Bianco
1994 Jepson Vineyards Chateau d'Alicia
1993 Navarro Vineyards Late Harvest White Riesling Cluster Select
1991 Navarro Vineyards Cabernet Sauvignon
1992 Obester Winery Zinfandel Gemello 60th Anniversary
1992 Fetzer Vineyards, Zinfandel Barrel Select
1993 Gabrielli Winery, Pinot Noir
1993 Domaine St. Gregory, Pinot Noir
1993 Navarro Vineyards, Pinot Noir, Methode a L'Ancienne
1993 Greenwood Ridge Vineyards, Merlot, Anderson Valley
1991 Parducci Wine Cellars, Charbono
1994 Handley Cellars, Pinot Meunier, "Pinot Mystere"

Once you've read through Blue's columns, turn your attention to the other wine columnists in the Blue on Wine and More subforum. Then turn your attention to Culinary Wine News, Reviews & Events. Here you'll find wonderful writing about wine and food, even the likes of comments on The Bridges of Madison County and hints on how to do a Bridges of Madison County party complete with Fiestaware for that Midwestern touch. Bev Bennett, a columnist for the Los Angeles Times points out that the movie is as much about food as it is about romance and how people are just as willing to define themselves by what they eat and how food is used to love and nurture as well as to even seduce their loved ones. Wow, and you thought is was just about Meryl Streep and Clint Eastwood dancing to old radio tunes!

Don't ignore the Microsoft Network's many other wine chat groups (such as the Wine Cellar and the Wine Cellar Guide), files you can download and read at your leisure (such as MS Wine Guide on the Web), and folders containing discussion on organic wines and barley wines. You can find all these in the list that's generated when you use the Find feature and search on the keyword *wine*.

FROM A REVIEW BY BEV BENNET FROM THE LOS ANGELES TIMES

In case you haven't noticed, food, soft music, and candlelight tend to go together nicely. Here's a sample from "From Bev Bennett Viewing the Culinary Scene in Bridges (Bridges of Madison County) published in the *Los Angeles Times*.

Two Iowa caterers discovered just how interwoven the food and story line were when they did the food styling for last year's movie starring Meryl Streep and Clint Eastwood. When filming began during the fall of 1994, the producers wanted local cooks, familiar with Iowa farm food of 30 years ago, to prepare dishes for several scenes in the movie.

Channing Work, the movie's production assistant, was in charge of finding the food talent. He turned to his sister Courtney, an artist and former caterer living in Des Moines. She asked Jane Hemminger, her catering partner who is now a food consultant, to join her. They auditioned with their Apple Brown Betty. The aroma of the baked apple and brown sugar dessert put the cast in character. It was a homey, comforting dish that Streep enjoyed.

"Apple Brown Betty got us the job," said Hemminger, who with Work wrote The Recipes of Madison County (Oxmoor House), a cookbook that contains recipes for each scene along with contemporary menus for family and guests.

The movie was filmed in Cumming, Iowa, in an abandoned farmhouse without running water or electricity. Hemminger and Work cooked in Des Moines, a 15-minute drive, and rushed hot food to the set three times a week or more. The women had to cook enough food to last for several takes of a scene, and they did: 30 pounds of mashed potatoes, trays of Apple Brown Betty. Fortunately, the crew scrambled for the leftovers.

COMPUSERVE WINE OFFERINGS

What does CompuServe have to offer? The gold mine on this service is the Bacchus Wine & Beer forum and the libraries it contains. Bacchus was the god of wine, and the forum is operated by Bacchus Data Services. It's the home for discussion of all beverages on CompuServe, and it's where you can find specific information about wine. The forum contains 23 libraries, which cover a broad range of topics including wine, beer, pipes, cigars, and more. Here's a brief review of some of the libraries that contain information about wine.

News/Forum Tools/Business is the how-to area where you can get instruction about using libraries, dealing with compressed files, and other forum business. It's a good place to stop the first time you enter any new forum on CompuServe.

Tasting Notes is your place to let people know what you think about the latest great bottle you've sampled. It's the no-pretense place, ready for discussions of any and everything regarding wines.

General Wine contains files of general interest as well as the most recent 12 monthly issues of *The Wine Investor/Buyer's Guide*, a wine newsletter. You can even get instructions on how to get a free issue of this internationally respected magazine.

When it comes time to shop, the Wine Shopping library will give you the information you need to buy wisely.

More information and newsletters provided by wineries and CompuServe members can be found in the Winery Info/ Newsletters library.

If you want information on computer programs that will help you organize your wine cellar, the Cellars/Cellaring library offers such and more. Not only are commercial programs reviewed and discussed, the site has (try before you buy) shareware and advice and construction tips for wine lovers who are thinking about buying or building their own cellar.

Is there anyone who doesn't need a tip now and then about wine? Both basic and advanced questions can be answered through the Wine Answers Library. Want to know about the classification system for French wines? How about whether wine corks really do breathe? You can read about these picks and many more.

The Winemaking & Grapes library contains information about growing wine grapes and making wine, including articles, techniques, and supply sources. As usual, anything that other CompuServe members can contribute is most welcome.

INTERNET WINE OFFERINGS

If you love wine, you'll love what the Internet has to offer for the beginner as well as the most serious of wine lovers. From seminars in Tokyo to guided tours of small wineries in the Unites States and elsewhere, you can visit, buy, and almost taste what's offered.

THE BEST GENERAL WINE PAGES

THE WINE PAGE (http://www.speakeasy.org/~winepage/wine.html)

You want a beginning place to be as complete as possible, and that's what The Wine Page, shown below, can offer you. You can begin with some Words about Wine, which will introduce you to this resource including comments and reviews by wine enthusiasts (and not necessarily professionals) such as Jarret Paschal's ideas about red wines and how they should be served.

This home page is just full of information, including reviews by the noted wine expert Robert Parker, *MacVine Magazine*, a tour of Washington State wines, and links to other wine pages. Once you read Parker's reviews, you can then rate his reviews—all in good fun.

SERVING WINE (from `http://www.speakeasy.org/~winepage/wine.html`)

What Next?

I chose to mention these three stories not so much to complain about wine in restaurants—most journalists in print publications can be relied upon to recycle those kinds of stories every six months or so. Instead, I wanted to shed light on what should be a "solvable problem" and hopefully encourage change. Compared to the most common complaints like cost and availability—issues which are often far more complex than the general public realizes—temperature should be pretty easy to address. In fact, all three of the restaurants detailed in the scenarios above have, in my opinion, outstanding lists and quite reasonable prices. Still, I can't recommend them to others based on my experiences.

Color me naive and innocent, but I refuse to believe that a restaurant staff capable of sourcing and assembling obscure ingredients into compelling and intricate menu items cannot figure out how to serve wine at a reasonable temperature. Until such time, I'm inclined to agree with the individual below who invited me over for dinner last week:

We should go out to dinner and drink some good wines…. On second thought, why don't you just come over to our house and we'll cook. That way, we don't have to hassle with restaurants and wine.

Seems reasonable enough to me, no?

WINES ON THE INTERNET (`http://www.wines.com/`)

Wines on the Internet has won several awards for their home page, and a quick glance should tell you why. It's nicely designed, easy to read and use, and full of information. The following page shows just a partial list of the links that it contains and where they take you.

The New Wine Press (`http://www.wines.com/winepress/press.html`) is a magazine offering articles by food and wine writers.

If you are looking for exceptional values in wines or want to visit a collection of wineries, try Virtual Wine Country (`http://www.wines.com/tasttop.html`).

The most fun on this page is the link to WineWizard's Resourcery with the Wine Quiz Question of the Week (by Jeff Isbrandtsen, developer of Arborware Wine Lover's Software), the Wine Lover's Reference, and the WineWizard's Introduction to popular wines.

The Official WebSite of

VINEYARD&WINERY
MANAGEMENT

North America's most complete resource
for growers and vintners.

VWM-ONLINE IS HERE!

Wineries | Village Shops | Tasting Room | Wine Events | WinePress | WineWizard

wine reviews & awards

- Best Buy of the Week: Mead On Wine

- Winners of the International Eastern Wine Competition

- Wine Words by M. Howie

features for wine lovers

- Cool Label-of-the-Month

- New Issue of the Wine Trader Magazine

- The Wine Trader Wine & Health Report

- This Month's Opinion Poll is About Corks

- Our Searchable Database of Wine Knowledge

- A Little Wine Quiz Question-of-the-Week

- Special Interest for Wine Enthusiasts

Want to know anything about wine? Try Wine Q&A on Wines on the Internet

Q. We received a bottle of 1980 Silver Oak cabernet sauvignon from a friend for our then new-born daughter's birth. My question is should we open it now, wait, or is it already too late?

A. Silver Oak was started in 1972 and spent its first decade housed in the old Oakville Dairy (which is where the 1980 was made). In 1992, Silver Oak purchased the Lyeth Winery in the Alexander Valley. All Silver Oak Cabernets are 100% Cabernet Sauvignon and aged in American oak for 3 years prior to bottling. The 1980 should have reached its height. Drink it up and enjoy the memory of your daughter's arrival. Then again, she's a teenager, and the realities of those difficult years might sometimes make the consumption of a good bottle of wine a necessity!

Just a last note about Wines on the Internet. If you're looking for a wine-related activity or an event, try the CyberCalendar of Wine Events (http://www.wines.com/events1.html) with listings organized by state and, of course, where it's all happening in wine, California.

AMERICAN WINE (http://www.foodwine.com/food/wine/)

American Wine is a really "clean" page, meaning that you can see the links to other pages easily and quickly get an idea where those links lead, but don't be fooled by this simple design. Behind the main headings and on the opening page, as you can see on the opposite page, is an extensive collection of information, and especially expert opinion, about wines.

Columns and Features offers a welcome from the editor, Gerry Troy, as well as columns such as The Wine Newbie, and the Wine Quiz. Frequently updated news included Just In! stories such as the success of a recent harvest, obituaries, and wine festivals. Competition Bulletin Board lists upcoming competitions, such as the Colorado State Fair and the San Diego National Wine Competition, and results. Regional Wine Country Reports takes you right to the source of what's happening and includes reviews of recently released wines as well as listings of best buys. Finally, *Services of American Wine Magazine* (which has this electronic edition on the Internet) offers the contents of the print medium online, including letters to the editor, a glossary of wine varietals, the American Wine Art Gallery, and guidance for beginners. This is a stunning page and perhaps the only place you need to stop.

Volume 2, 1996

 Welcome to the oldest, most critically acclaimed wine magazine on the Internet. We have designed **American Wine** to load quickly while providing maximum information in an attractive, clean, easily-navigated format.

Click on the button of your choice to enter the world of *AMERICAN* Wine.

Table of Contents

Columns and Features

Frequently Updated News

Regional Wine Country Reports

Services of American Wine

In the Table of Contents and text, you may click on any of the highlighted text to see related information. By clicking on pictures with blue borders, you can see expanded versions. Depending upon your computer, please allow a minute or so for the expanded picture to develop.

 American Wine on the Web has been rated among the top 5% of all sites on the Internet by Point Survey.

TAKE A TRIP: VISITING WINERIES

If you can't leave home to get there, the best thing is to do it virtually. That's exactly what the following Web sites offer: a sort of virtual trip.

NAPA VALLEY VIRTUAL VISIT (http://www.napavalley.com/cgi-bin/home.o)

This page really is just like a tour, and you can be your own guide. There's even a moving message across the bottom of the screen to greet you and encourage you to go to certain places in Napa! You can select Current Events, Sightseeing & Activities, Lodging & Spas, Dining & Delis, Shopping, Golf, or areas such as

Calistoga, St. Helena, Yountville. Then you can shop a bit, and even look into renting space and equipment for a party.

The best feature of the page, however, is that you can go to the home page of over 30 Napa Wineries or search for particular winery from a series of categories such as family owned wineries, production, and off the beaten path. If you want to know about wine in this fertile part of California, try this page.

NAPA VALLEY WINERIES (http://www.freerun.com/napavalley/mwinerie.html)

This page is an extension of the Napa Virtual Visit page we just described. More Napa wineries can be found here, and you can even click on a map (see next page) and find out what's there and how to get there. As you can see, the map is full of locations rich in experiences regarding wine, from the **Chardonnay Golf Club** (http://www.napavalley.com/napavalley/outdoor/chargolf/chargolf.html) to the **Wine Country Inn.** (http://www.napavalley.com/napavalley/lodging/inns/wcinn/index.html).

VISIT UPSTATE NEW YORK
(http://www.spinners.com/tompcoliving/food2.html)

Cool nights and warm days make good grapes great, and that's what you'll find growing at Roger and Nancy Battistella's family-owned winery. At their Six Mile Creek Vineyard in Ithaca, New York, you can get a tour of the winery and taste some sample foods for sale. You can't taste the wines, but you can appreciate how this family started in the early 1980s with an idea and now bottle up to 4,000 gallons of wine each year. You can also find another 36 upstate New York wineries at http://fallcrk.tc.cornell.edu/Entertainment/Winefest/wineries.html, home of (no kidding) Days of Wine and Noses.

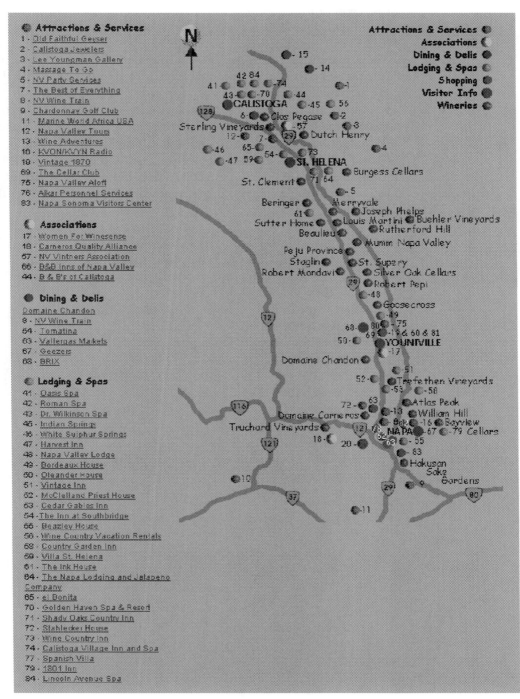

◐ Attractions & Services

1 - Old Faithful Geyser
2 - Calistoga Jewelers
3 - Lee Youngman Gallery
4 - Massage To Go
5 - NV Party Services
7 - The Best of Everything
8 - NV Wine Train
9 - Chardonnay Golf Club
11 - Marine World Africa USA
12 - Napa Valley Tours
13 - Wine Adventures
18 - KVON/KVYN Radio
19 - Vintage 1870
69 - The Cellar Club
75 - Napa Valley Aloft
76 - Alkar Personnel Services
83 - Napa Sonoma Visitors Center

◖ Associations

17 - Women For Winesense
18 - Carneros Quality Alliance
57 - NV Vintners Association
66 - B&B Inns of Napa Valley
44 - B & B's of Calistoga

● Dining & Delis

Domaine Chandon
8 - NV Wine Train
64 - Tomatina
63 - Vallergas Markets
67 - Geezers
68 - BRIX

◑ Lodging & Spas

41 - Oasis Spa
42 - Roman Spa
43 - Dr. Wilkinson Spa
46 - Indian Springs
46 - White Sulphur Springs
47 - Harvest Inn
48 - Napa Valley Lodge
49 - Bordeaux House
50 - Oleander House
51 - Vintage Inn
52 - McClelland Priest House
63 - Cedar Gables Inn
54 - The Inn at Southbridge
66 - Beazley House
56 - Wine Country Vacation Rentals
68 - Country Garden Inn
59 - Villa St. Helena
61 - The Ink House
64 - The Napa Lodging and Jalapeno Company
65 - el Bonita
70 - Golden Haven Spa & Resort
71 - Shady Oaks Country Inn
72 - Stahlecker House
73 - Wine Country Inn
74 - Calistoga Village Inn and Spa
77 - Spanish Villa
79 - 1801 Inn
84 - Lincoln Avenue Spa

Attractions & Services ◐
Associations ◖
Dining & Delis ●
Lodging & Spas ◑
Shopping ◐
Visitor Info ●
Wineries ◐

N

15
14
42 84
74
41
1
43 70 44
45 56
CALISTOGA
128
6
Clos Pegase
2
Sterling Vineyards
57
3
12
7
29
Dutch Henry
46
65
73
4
47 59
54
ST. HELENA
Burgess Cellars
St. Clement
71 64
5
Beringer
Merryvale
61
Joseph Phelps
Sutter Home
Louis Martini
Buehler Vineyards
Beaulieu
Rutherford Hill
Mumm Napa Valley
Peju Province
Staglin
St. Supery
Robert Mondavi
Silver Oak Cellars
29
Robert Pepi
48
Goosecross
12
49
68
80
75
69
19 & 60 & 81
50
YOUNTVILLE
17
Domaine Chandon
51
52
Trefethen Vineyards
53
58
116
63
Atlas Peak
72
19
William Hill
Domaine Carneros
16
Bayview
Truchard Vineyards
121
78
84
NAPA
67
79 Cellars
18
63
55
121
20
63
83
Hakusan Sake Gardens
10
29
9
37
80
11

LISTS AND LISTS

There are hundreds of lists on the Internet, all offering their own version of heaven to the wine drinker who is looking for exactly the right bottle. These pages are for browsing and exploring what's out there. Many let you order right over the Web; others are restricted by law. Most offer a selection of a few wines broken down by category such as Chardonnay, Other White Wines, Sparkling Wines, Cabernet Sauvignon, and Other Red Wines, whereas some focus on a particular wine. Many are restaurant lists—possibly helping you determine where you eat based on the house list.

The most ambitious link to other wineries is HandiLinks to Wineries (http://www.ahandyguide.com/cat1/w/w54.htm), which consists of over 150 links to other wineries and provides the opportunity to add your own or a wine link that you know of that is not on their list.

Then you can browse these until something strikes you for type, quality, price, or year:

- Porcini Restaurant in Chicago (http://dine.package.com/chicago/porcini/wine.html),
- Arthur's Restaurant in Santa Clara, California (http://bonviv.com/ home/arthurs/winelst.htm),
- Larocca's in Tucson, Arizona (http://www.ibs-net.com/tucson/rest/ larocca4.htm), and
- The Wine House (http://www.virtually.com/plaza/winehouse/champagne.html), a retailer of fine wines where you can order online.

CHOCOLATE

Chocolate on America Online

•

Chocolate on CompuServe

•

Chocolate on Microsoft Network

•

Chocolate on the Internet

•

Recipes and Stores Galore

When I did my first search for online sites that have something to do with chocolate, AltaVista returned more than *76,000* hits. If you think that's an indication of how popular chocolate is and how much people love to eat it, cook and bake with it, and just think about it, you're absolutely right.

Chocolate comes from the cocoa bean (the fruit of the cocoa tree) which grows in warm, semitropical climates. The beans are harvested, cleaned, roasted, and shelled (revealing the "nib" or meat), and processed where the chocolate liquor (which is unsweetened) is extracted, cocoa fat (removed at first from the nib) added back in, tempered and voila, you've got heaven.

In a futile attempt to justify why chocolate is so delicious and why they can't live without it either, scientists have discovered it has some of the addictive properties of illicit drugs and even produces endorphins (those hormones associated with feelings of overwhelming love). Be that as it may, what follows is what you can find, and where you can find it, about chocolate online. If you want to know a lot more about the history of chocolate and its characteristics, visit the Godiva homepage at (`http://www.godiva.com/resources/history.html`) or Bill Cupp's homepage (`http://www.rmc.ca/~cupp/thought1.htm#chocolate`).

CHOCOLATE ON AMERICA ONLINE

As you have seen, America Online has lots of good information on cooking, but not much on chocolate. All that's available are some commercial sites such as Godiva (expensive and OK) and 1-800-FLOWERS, who make up baskets with chocolates.

CHOCOLATE ON COMPUSERVE

Remember the Better than Sex cake from our discussion on deserts? Perhaps you thought a name a bit strange? In the Cook's Forum in CompuServe, search the library and enter the key word chocolate and you'll find even more—Kid-Pleasin' Moon Cake, Chocolate Oatmeal Cookies, Killer Brownies (don't forget to freeze then eat them cold), and finally Chocolate Kahlua Fantasy Cake Cioppino's (reprinted from *Gourmet* magazine).

CHOCOLATE, CHOCOLATE, CHOCOLATE

Want to know how much America loves chocolate? (from the National Confectioners Association and the Chocolate Manufacturers Association at http://www.candyusa.org/stats.html)

- On average, each American ate 11.5 pounds of chocolate in 1995. That's over 3 billion pounds total.
- The retail chocolate industry in the U.S. is worth $13 billion per year.
- Valentine's Day still means chocolate. Americans spend $665 million each Valentine's Day on candy, making it the fourth biggest holiday of the year for confectionery purchases (after Halloween, Christmas, and Easter).
- American men say they'd rather receive chocolate than flowers on Valentine's Day, especially those over the age of 50. Sixty-eight percent of men age 50 or older say they'd prefer receiving chocolate over flowers from their sweetheart on Valentine's Day, while just 22% said they'd rather have the flowers.
- The first "chocolate box" was introduced by Richard Cadbury in 1868, when he decorated a candy box with a painting of his young daughter holding a kitten in her arms. Cadbury also invented the first Valentine's Day candy box.
- Chocolate manufacturers use 40% of the world's almonds, 20% of the world's peanuts and 8% of the world 's sugar. Members of the Chocolate Manufacturers Association use about 3.5 million pounds of the whole milk each day to make milk chocolate.

Enough said.

CHOCOLATE ON MICROSOFT NETWORK

Microsoft Network offers the most of the three big boards, with the Passions and Chocolate Drinks folders. If you look at the Chocolate folder within Passions, you'll find more then 100 conversations about chocolate including comments, ideas, recipes, and just talk about the sweet. There's Chocolate Damnation, Chocolate Biscotti, Frozen Hot Chocolate (yep!), Chocolate Lush, and, of course, The Ultimate Brownie (as if everyone's favorite brownie recipe is not the ultimate!).
You can end up your Microsoft Network tour with a visit to Pilou's Chat Room and hundreds of recipes from the Hershey's chocolate people from Hershey, Pennsylvania where the street lights are shaped like Hershey's kisses (really).

Microsoft Network User in Need of Help (Actual Posts on Microsoft Network!)
What do you do when you REALLY REALLY REALLY crave something really " " " " " chocolatey, but you don't want any fat and not too many calories???? Help!!! I'm dying!
Erica

And the answers:

Hi Erica,
I usually make a cup of hot chocolate, using "dutched" cocoa (such as Bensdorp's), with skim milk, a scant 1/2 teaspoon of sugar, and two BIG marshmallows (no fat in marshmallows, although there are calories). Anything else I can think of has lots more calories. :(
I'm sure other folks have some ideas, too!
Perry

I call it 2222 - two tablespoons butter, 2 tblp. cocoa powder, 2 tbl. sugar, 2 tbl. milk. Mix sugar, butter, cocoa in sauce pan, on medium heat stir until all melted together, couple min., then take off heat and stir in milk. You can add nuts if you want . I grab a spoon and gooooooooooooo! A finger works just as well! Anyway it's a quick fix.

oooo — a LADY AFTER MY OWN HEART! Hot chocolate with a dash of caramel flavor, or maple, or butternut, or coconut, or peanut butter flavorings.... Or, for the low cal treat — but you lose some flavor, :(, try using about half the amount of cocoa called for in your cup. Build the flavor back up with Chocolate Flavoring, and hide the weakness with one of the above. Fewer calories, less fat, less chocolate zonk. Other chocolate craving help — hard candy made with chocolate flavorings.
    ^ ^
  ='.'=

CHOCOLATE ON THE INTERNET

Most people would be content just to have their Nestle's chips to munch on and an occasional hot chocolate made with a fine ground sweet chocolate such as Giardelli. But the folks who have gone online, including the commercial establishments, go far beyond the simple. While most of what is online is commercial (stores and companies selling things), even those Web pages are delightful. Then there's the "I can't live without my chocolate crowd" who also have their own home pages.

MRS. FIELDS COOKIES

(from the Passion Folder on Microsoft Network)

You've always wanted it and here it is.

Mrs. Field's Chocolate Chip Cookies
Yield: 55 servings
1 c butter
1 c brown sugar
1 c sugar
2 eggs
1 tsp vanilla
2 c flour
2½ c oatmeal*
½ tsp salt
1 tsp baking soda
1 tsp baking powder
12 oz chocolate chips
8 oz hershey bar; grated
1½ c nuts; pecans or walnuts
Cream butter and sugars. Add eggs and vanilla. Mix oatmeal*, salt, baking soda and baking powder. Mix all ingredients together and add chips, candy and nuts. Bake on ungreased cookie sheets (Cushion Aire-insulated won't burn cookies). Make golf-ball size cookies, spaced 2" apart. Bake at 375 degrees for 6 minutes. Makes 112 cookies.

* Oatmeal: put small amounts of oatmeal into blender on high until it turns to powder. Measure first, then blend.

GENERAL CHOCOLATE PAGES

There aren't many, but there are some great ones such as The Chocolate Lover's Page (http://bc.emanon.net/chocolate/) you see on the next page. These 16 pages of chocolate related resources cover everything from ordering imported chocolates from Belgium and Finland, personalized chocolates and novelties, chocolate covered cactus and chiles, cakes including Chocolate Ecstasy, chocolate covered potato chips, elephant heads made of chocolate, and, finally, Panty-of-the-Month (which are not made with chocolate, but come with chocolates).

Besides this comprehensive listing of chocolate products, other chocolate resources are available from this page.

Since the passion for chocolate runs so high among its fans, you won't be surprised to find the The Quasi-Comprehensive Candy Bar Wrapper Image Archive of candy bar wrappers from Brad at http://www.math.okstate.edu/~kbradle/snacks/ which also has links to other wrapper collections. If you have a sound card, you can hear Brad's greeting and rationale for why he even created the homepage in the first place. It's well worth the visit. And if you like the wrapper collection you see here, you can visit several others such as Roberto's (http://www.infinet.com/~rbatina/other/candy.html) listing hundreds and hundreds (but no graphics) such as Charms Blow Pops (in all the flavors), Flake (Australia), Marabou (Sweden), and Reber Mozart Kugeln (from Germany).

You can learn other people's opinions about different brands of chocolate and the goings on in the chocolate word at Chocolate Talk (http://www.kaiwan.com/~perew/choctalk.html) and Cloister's Chocolate Review Page (http://www.hhhh.org/cloister/chocolate/). Chocolate Talk authored by Mark Perew is fun, since each use of the word chocolate takes you to another chocolate link such as the perfect chocolate at Sweet Seductions (http://connexion. parallax.co.uk/seduct/). The Chocolate Review Page provides that crucial information about buying fine chocolates such as Valrhona's Noir Amer—one of the best chocolates this page's author ever tasted. It has upwards of 70% cocoa solids and is first in the ingredients list (whereas your run-of-the-mill candy bar has less than 20% solids and lots of junk besides). This must powerful stuff. The review themselves are available at (`http://www.hhhh.org/ cloister/chocolate/reviews/`) and list 13 brands (such as Hershey's, Ibarra, and Lindt) and more than three times that many reviews of different products produced by type, and other manufacturers. If you want to know what other people think about chocolate, this is the place to visit.

Another great starting point is The Chocolate Club (`http://www.idma.com/chocolate/`) with links to chocolate sites, events, and a recipe archive with 75 entries. And yes, you can become a member of The Chocolate Club and for $17.95 a month, receive a one pound selection from among the 2000 chocolatiers in the United States.

And finally, who could resist the link to the top 20 reasons why chocolate is better than sex at `http://www.writepage.com/ chocolat.htm`? We'll make you go there to find out since some of them are a bit off-color.

PERSONAL CHOCOLATE HOMEPAGES

There aren't many of these, but what's there is fun, informative and useful.

The most informative is Pam Williams (`http://studio.bpe.com/ food/recipes/hotchoc/two.html`), Hot Chocolate which includes Chocolate Tidbits (history and a perspective on where chocolate fits into our food world), Chocolate Makers Extraordinary (a visit with fabulous chocolate makers such as Callebaut), The Traveling Chocoholic (reader's favorite chocolate shops and events), and The Literary Chocoholic (books, articles any more on chocolate). And with each new issue, there's recipe such as Chocolate Ganache (Lesson Two) and recipes to accompany the new lesson as well.

I Need My CHOCOLATE! (`http://www.qrc.com/~sholubek/ choco/start.htm`) from Shellie Holubek is full of interesting and unique links such as Fargo's Iced Mocha (using heavy cream) at (`http://www.qrc.com/~sholubek/choco/dcchoco.htm#fargo`) and a listserv which you can subscribe to and insure that you will receive recipes on a monthly basis. You can find out about the listserve at `http://www.qrc.com/~sholubek/choco/majrdomo.htm`. And you can also find a link here to rec.food.chocolate, the major newsgroup devoted to chocolate in all its forms.

Dawn's home page (`http://www.hcc.cc.fl.us/services/staff/dawn/choco.htm`) can greet you with a .wav sound file ("Would you like a piece of chocolate?") but can also take you to a host of commercial links, but with some helpful (but of course, opinionated) commentary such as Ben & Jerry's (`http://www.benjerry.com/indexg.html`) ("Oh, I just love that Chunky Monkey," Dawn says.).

RECIPES AND STORES GALORE

We didn't put chocolate recipes in the section titled Recipes, since we thought that chocolate was such a special food, it deserved its own place. But, don't forget some of the good recipe search engines such as AltaVista and Lycos and that almost every chocolate company has its own home page such as Hershey (`http://www.hersheys.com`), Nestle (`http://www.nestle.com/`) and the Ethel M. Chocolates Company (`http://www.ethelm.com/`). You can find an extensive list of companies that produce chocolate (and other kinds of candies) at `http://www.candyusa.org/store.html`, the home page page for the National Confectioners Association.

The majority of entries on the Internet about chocolate are recipes in one form or another and links to commercial sites. Keep in mind that even if a page seems extensive in its coverage and offering doesn't mean that it is all-inclusive. There is always that one other connection that one page has, which the other doesn't, which might be exactly the one you are looking for. So, unless you find what you want, search a little more.

The Chocolate Lovers Page, which we mentioned above, has an extensive listing of stores and companies that sell chocolate online and it would seem unlikely that you would not be able to find a vendor that sells what you want.

The Candy Store Company Links

Adams & Brooks

American Licorice Company

Ben Myerson Candy Co.

Bobs Candies, Inc.

Brown & Haley

Clark Bar America Inc.

Ethel M Chocolate

Glade Candy Co.

Yahoo (http://www.yahoo.com/Business_and_Economy/Companies/Food/Snacks/Candy/Chocolate/) also has multipage listing of companies with some rather unique contribution such as X-Rated Chocolates (http://www.eden.com/~plainwrp/choco/) offering chocolate with adult themes and the R.M. Palmer company offering chocolate novelties for Christmas and Easter.

You can find company cookbooks such as the Hershey's (http://www.hersheys.com/) and the Online Cookbook at (http://www.hersheys.com/recipes/chocolate.pasta.recipes.html) including recipes for beverages, breads, cakes, frostings, candy, cookies, desserts, hints, pies, and a recipes for today plus a

TIPS FROM
ADVENTURES IN DINING
http://www.go-dining.
com/recipes.html

When cooking chocolate, remember to keep the heat low and gentle and the chocolate dry. Melt chocolate using indirect heat, as with a double boiler or a metal bowl set over water. Be sure to keep the temperature below 120F and don't let the water simmer. Too much heat can scorch the chocolate, creating an unpleasant flavor, while the steam created by the water or any moisture will cause the chocolate to stiffen or "seize," ruining the consistency. To control the temperature, let the water steam, then lower the heat before placing the bowl or double boiler on top. The residual heat will be sufficient to melt the chocolate.

wonderful selection of holiday recipes. You can even take an informative tour of the factory (sorry no more real-person tours conducted at the real factory).

Other good recipe sites are Delicious Chocolate Recipes (http://www.go-dining.com/recipes.html) from *Adventures in Dining Magazine* featuring Chocolate Cream Pie and Chocolate Soufflé (be careful!) and a very nice introduction to the history of chocolate and some tips on how to cook with it.

More rich recipes are available from Christopher's Recipes (http://www.christophers.com/hotncold.html) from the restaurant including Chocolate Ice Cream, Dark Chocolate Sauce, and a Chocolate Tart.

HOLIDAY AND FESTIVAL FOODS

Holiday and Festival Foods on America Online
•
Holiday and Festival Foods on CompuServe
•
Holiday and Festival Foods on Microsoft Network
•
Holiday and Festival Foods on the Internet

It doesn't matter much which holidays you celebrate, they always tend to be accompanied by food. Whether it be Christmas Pudding, Hanukah Latkes, Thanksgiving Pumpkin Pie, or Mardi Gras King Cake, the special time of the year makes these special foods even more delicious. The online world brings us a somewhat scattered collection of food resources, with the big boards (America Online, CompuServe, and the Microsoft Network) actually providing more than the Internet (just about the only time that happens). Also, for the most part, the information available online about food is mixed in with information about the history of the holiday, how it's celebrated, and other ancillary aspects of the celebration.

Keep in mind that holidays are seasonal. For that reason, when you search for information about a holiday or a particular type of food or recipe, if it is not the season, you will probably find last year's contribution, if anything. This is especially true of commercial online services and newsgroups.

HOLIDAY AND FESTIVAL FOODS ON AMERICA ONLINE

You can find complete Holiday kitchen recipes and tips in the *Woman's Day* area on America Online (keyword: *woman's*) for at least Christmas and Thanksgiving (see opposite page). The *Woman's Day* Christmas area features a listing of recipes (such as Snowflake cookies and Holly Wreath Cake), instructions for making garlands, and the *1995 Cookie Cookbook* (with a new one probably appearing soon).

Perfect gravy can be yours through the Thanksgiving Feasts as well as recipes for Creole Mixed Vegetables and Angel Biscuits. If you're not sure what to serve on Thanksgiving, America Online and *Woman's Day* offer recipes for a traditional Thanksgiving dinner consisting of Roast Turkey with Pecan Bread Stuffing, Perfect Gravy, and Crunch Cranberry Relish. You have to think up the vegetables and desserts, but that should be no problem because such is available in the same *Woman's Day* forum.

In America Online, don't forget to check the Monthly Menus feature within the *Woman's Day* Kitchen, where you can look to the month of the holiday (such as November for Thanksgiving) and find helpful suggestions.

Information about Hanukah and other Jewish holidays is available in the Jewish Community forum (keyword: *Jewish*). Here you'll find information about the most recent (or soon to come) holiday. When we signed on, there was a nice spread about Succoth, the festival of the fall harvest where many Jews eat out of doors under a canopy of branches, much as they would have while harvesting in the fields some 6,000 years ago.

The Holiday and Festival Foods folder in the Jewish Community forum contains recipes for Chanukah (the festival of lights), Rosh Hashanah (the Jewish New Year), Passover (celebration of the exodus from slavery), Purim (feast of the Tabernacles), and Shabbat (the weekly celebration welcoming the Sabbath). Clicking on any one of these folders (such as Chanukah) reveals recipes for that holiday. For example, the Hanukah recipes include Potato Latkes (what else?), Cheese Pie, No Fry Lacy Potato Pancakes, Sweet Potato Latkes, and Sufganiot (Israeli jelly doughnuts).

HOLIDAY AND FESTIVAL FOODS ON COMPUSERVE

The best location for finding food-related information as well as recipes about any holiday is in *The Better Homes* Kitchen (**Find**: *better homes*) and the Cooks forum. The *Better Homes* Kitchen area features monthly topics such as Thanksgiving for November; Christmas, Hanukah, and Kwanza for December; and Easter in the spring. Also, there's a forum attached to the *Better Homes* area that you can enter and discuss different topics. Don't pass up the other areas of the *Better Homes* Kitchen such as New, Prize Winning Recipes, and Bonus. There's always something well worth looking at.

HOLIDAY AND FESTIVAL FOODS ON THE MICROSOFT NETWORK

The Microsoft Network has several nice holiday features including a Christmas download-and-run file. Use the **Find** feature and search on *Christmas cooking* to see the well-planned series of events including online workshops in making cookies and desserts for the holidays as well as chocolates and decorations. There's also a link to a chat room of Christmas matters and one to a collection of recipes as well.

Other holidays have equally attractive collections of information. The Jewish Holiday Folder has collections of recipes for the High Holidays, Chanukah, Purim, and Passover, and there is a handy Thanksgiving Planner from Baarns Software that you can download. It's an Excel application where you enter the number of people you plan on having for the feast, click on the categories of food you'll be serving, and the planner does the rest. It can even print out a detailed ingredients list such as you see on the opposite page. This is such a complete Thanksgiving planner that it does everything but cook the turkey!

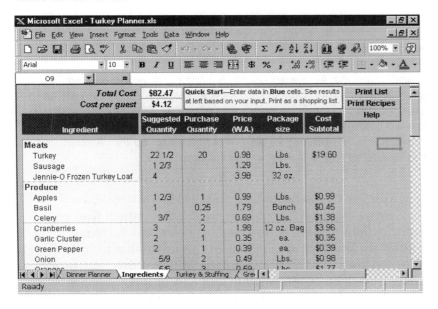

HOLIDAY AND FESTIVAL FOODS ON THE INTERNET

The Internet is mostly filled with recipes for holidays and festivals, but there are a few good and general home pages as places to start.

GENERAL PAGES

Start with Cooking for the Holidays (`http://www.bpe.com/food/recipes/corn/holiday.html`), a home page sponsored by BPE, an Internet company. This home page is part of Sally's Place (`http://www.bpe.com/index.html`), a delightfully designed food-related home page that is full of resources. The Cooking for the Holidays page gives general advice that changes with the season. For example, around Thanksgiving you can find a recipe for Maple-Orange Wild Rice, a wonderful accompaniment to Turkey or other poultry. Accompanying the recipe is also a discussion of the main ingredient (such as wild rice) and tips on buying (get the longest and blackest wild rice you can find—usually from Minnesota or California).

WHAT IS KWANZA?

(from the publisher HarperCollins at `http://www.harpercollins.com/kids/kwan.htm`)

While a relatively new celebration on the American scene, Kwanza is a seven-day American festival based upon the celebration of seven principles called the Nguzo Saba, one for each day; unity, self-determination, working together, supporting each other, purpose, creativity, and faith. Kwanza is celebrated once a year, and was created by Dr. Maulana Karenga, a civil rights activist. Kwanza means "first fruits" in Swahili, words chosen so that African Americans would remember that all of Africa is their ancestral land.

Another excellent starting point is Happy 3 Holidays (`http://www.harpercollins.com/kids/holi.htm`), which features information, recipes, and related activities for Christmas, Hanukah, and Kwanza. For those of us unfamiliar with the rituals for food associated with any of these holidays, this page provides some introductory information and easy to follow recipes.

What's a traditional Kwanza food? Benne Cakes, a sesame seed (for good luck) cookie. Look for the recipe at `http://www.harpercollins.com/kids/kwan.htm#c`.

The other two holidays on the Happy 3 Holidays home page are Hanukah and Christmas. The Hanukah information (`http://www.harpercollins.com/kids/hanu.htm`) takes you through the same type of information as that presented about Kwanza, including what the holiday is, when the holiday is celebrated, and what some of the rituals are. The big deal on Hanukah is fried foods to commemorate the use of oil to light the temple that was destroyed and then rebuilt. The miracle of the holiday is that a small amount of oil burned for eight days (the length of the holiday).

So people who celebrate Hanukah cook in oil, the most traditional and common dish being potato pancakes or latkes. As you might expect, there are as many recipes for latkes as there are Jewish grandmothers. We'll get to several of those later on in this section.

The Christmas (`http://www.harpercollins.com/kids/chri.htm`) holiday section for this home page follows a pattern much like the other two: a discussion of what the holiday is about, when it is celebrated, and so on. Many churches celebrate on days other than December 25, such as the Armenians who celebrate on January 18. Of course, there's a recipe from the well-known Laura Ingalls Wilder book *Little House on the Prairie*, Molasses-on-Snow-Candy.

BUTTERBALL

P R E S E N T S

Welcome back! You're at Butterball Online, your turkey headquarters on the Internet and the one place that surfing and stuffing go hand in hand. Last year, thousands of you visited us to learn how to prepare a picture-perfect turkey. Whether you're a seasoned veteran known for your lump-free gravy, or you don't know a drumstick from a chopstick, think of this website as an electronic grandmother -- ready to answer everything you ever wanted to know about roasting a turkey but were afraid to ask. By the way, this is definitely a bird for all seasons -- you'll get year-round ideas for whole turkeys, turkey sandwiches, turkey sausages, ground turkey, turkey cutlets, and lots more...Mmmmm! Can you smell that delicious aroma? It's from all of the delicious recipes we've included here for you. Enjoy!

NEW! **WIN A FREE SONY CAMCORDER!**

How to Prepare a Picture-Perfect Butterball Turkey!
We've stuffed this section full of recipes, carving tips, grilling ideas, FAQs, a peek inside the Butterball Turkey Talk-Line, and all kinds of practical advice, including "Ten Steps to a Picture-Perfect Turkey".

Recipes
Dozens of taste-tempting recipes! (And we're not just talking turkey -- we're talking side dishes, desserts, leftovers, make-ahead meals, regional favorites, grilling ideas, everyday recipes using ground turkey and fresh turkey cuts, low-fat recipes, new chicken recipes, and more...)

What's New from Butterball?
Chicken--yes, chicken! Find out about new "Chicken Requests." Exciting, delicious chicken in 5 tantalizing varieties--And they're baked, not fried.

Good for You! Eating Well With Butterball All Year Round
The low-down on just how low-fat turkey really is....and the skinny on some low-fat, low-calorie recipes using fresh ground turkey, turkey lunch meat and cutlets.

Just For Fun!
Nothing goes better with turkey than a good laugh -- so have one on us, along with a slice of turkey trivia...plus, if you've ever wanted to hear a real turkey gobble -- listen up...

Attention Journalists: Click here for the complete 1996 press kit!

Preparation | Recipe | What's New | Eating Well | Just for Fun | Home Page

This site is best viewed using Netscape 1.1 or higher.
This site was created by Edelman Public Relations Worldwide

WHAT ARE GIBLETS, ANYWAY?

(information about turkeys from The Butterball hotline at
`http://www.butterball.com/butterball/ turkey.html`)

Want leftovers? Carving tips? Information on grilling? You'll find it all at this home page, and even the phone number (800-323-4848) you can use to talk with the people at Butterball— and what stories they can tell. In the 15 years they've been operating, they're received almost 2 million calls and a many as 8,000 on Thanksgiving Day alone! This is an informative and fun site.

Who can approach Thanksgiving without thinking of Butterball Online (`http://www.butterball.com/`)? Shown on the previous page, this home page receives thousands of hits each day during the holiday season. Here you'll find the recipe for what they call a Picture-Perfect Butterball Turkey (and they have the picture to prove it at `http://www.butterball.com/butterball/ turkey.html`) including the ten steps you need to follow to make it so.

HOLIDAY AND FESTIVAL RECIPES

The first thing you'll need are ingredients, and you can find a description of special ones at Special Ingredients for Holiday Cooking (`http://www.byerlys.com/bbag/Nov1995/featured.html`), such as mascarpone cheese (essential for making tiramisu), meringue powder (for those gingerbread houses), and whole vanilla beans that are used to flavor sugar and custards. This home page is sponsored by Byerly's, the big food chain in the Upper Midwest, but you can get many of these ingredients at any well-stocked gourmet store or order many through the mail or online. Even if you can't get to a Byerly's, you can get to these ingredients. Look for sources for those ingredients in the next chapter, "Shopping Online."

What follows is a potpourri of just about everything, from the fancy pages containing lots of graphics to the bare minimum of text. But beware, all of these recipes sound wonderful and would be well worth exploring, if not trying.

Christmas Recipes (`http://holiday.ritech.com/christmas/ recipe.html`) is a three-page collection of recipes from the Christmas home page including 20 different recipes for baking, candy, and drinks. Each recipe, such as the one below, is one that is guaranteed to please the most discerning sweet tooth. You can also find a nice cookie recipe for Christmas Stars at

http://www.gil.com.au/ozkidz/Christmas/star.html.

RECIPE: SEVEN LAYER BARS
from http://holiday.ritech.com/christmas/recipes/layerbar.html

1 stick margarine
1 cup graham cracker crumbs
1 cup chocolate chips
1 cup coconut
1 cup butterscotch chips
1 cup nuts
1 can sweetened condensed milk

Melt margarine in 9 x 13-inch pan. Add graham cracker crumbs, pat lightly to make crust. Sprinkle with chips, nuts, and coconut. Pour can of milk over top. Bake at 350F for 20 to 30 minutes.

Christmas Stars

These are really easy to make and great for Christmas parties for young and old.

Ingredients:- 90 grams butter
1 and 1/4 cups plain flour
1 tablespoon water
1 teaspoon white vinegar
raspberry jam
beaten egg for glazing

Procedure:-

● Rub butter and flour together until finely crumbled.
● Combine water and vinegar and add to the crumbed mixture to make a firm dough. Lightly knead until smooth.
● Wrap and chill dough for about an hour.
● Then roll out dough onto a lightly floured surface. Roll out dough into a large square about 5 mm thick. Cut into 6 mm squares with a sharp knife.
● To shape, cut each square in the following way...from each point almost to the centre of each square.
● Dab the centre of each square with jam. Fold every other point in to meet the centre.
● Place on to a baking tray. Lightly glaze each star with beaten egg.
●Bake at 230 degrees c for 8-10 minutes
●Cool and Enjoy!

The Jewish holidays in general, such as the High Holy days consisting of Rosh Hashanah and Yom Kippur, which come on strong on the Internet at `http://www.jewish.com/bk950908/cook.htm`, and Passover (`http://www.bpe.com/food/recipes/fiszer/passover.html`), are all part of Sally's Place (`http://www.bpe.com/index.html`). Other sites for good Hanukah recipes are The Hanukah Pages (`http://www.jcn18.com/hanukkah/`), which are not only full of recipes but of things to do as well, and Hanukah (`http://www.bpe.com/food/recipes/fiszer/hanukah.html`).

Remember that holidays are seasonal, and you probably won't find current information on what you are looking for until 1 to 2 months before the holiday begins.

Finally, if you're looking for a festival to attend, point your browser at the Festival and Events home page (`http://www.w2.com/docs2/act/festivals/festivals.html`). This is a special events calendar that highlights festivals and food fairs such as the Oakdale, California, chocolate tasting, Hershey's chocolate tour festival, or the Santa Cruz annual clam chowder cookoff. Before you run off to attend, however, check the page for specifics as to time and dates.

SHOPPING ONLINE

Ingredients

•

Kitchen Equipment

•

Stores Online

•

Commercial Ventures on the Online Services

E ver wonder how those wonderful fruit tarts with the scalloped edges come out of the pan in one piece? The right equipment, that's how (a two-piece tart pan). What about those wonderfully uniform slices of tomato or cucumber? The right equipment again (a Mandolin). And those cool tall hats?

You certainly need to know your stuff to cook well, but you need the right tools to turn what you know into what you want it to be. Here's where you can find whatever you need, from a professional pizza pan to that $14,000 drop-in Gaggenau stove top (for the summer home of course). Most of these are home pages for companies that manufacture and/or sell cooking equipment at all levels, including both professional and consumer, as well as food companies selling directly to the consumer over the Internet.

INGREDIENTS

Need truffles for that special potato recipe? How about Tunisian spice mix? Or sun-ripened tomatoes? You can get these ingredients (which may or may not be at your local grocery), or information about them, right off the Internet.

You should begin your search for special ingredients with StarChefs (http://www.starchefs.com/secretingredients.html), which offers several pages of vendors who specialize in food ingredients that are unusual. Here's just a partial list.

- Truffles (from Urbanai Truffles USA)
- Stoneground Grits (from Old Virginia Byrd Mill)
- Beijing Blast (from Big Flavor Foods, Inc.)
- Sugar Cane (from Anriana's Caravan)
- Dried chilies, pickled chilies, and more chilies! (Mo Hotta Mo Betta)

You can get the street address and phone number for each of these, and several others, on the StarChef home page.

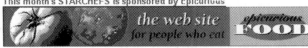

the web site for people who eat epicurious **FOOD**

SECRET INGREDIENTS

When you want to prepare a recipe but can't find that exotic or unusual ingredient we suggest that you look to our source list for assistance. We will provide you with helpful information and vendors of hard to find products so that you can make dishes as authentic as possible.

Secret Ingredients

Please scroll through the list below to see the vendors information. We are constantly adding new information so check back often!

KING ARTHUR FLOUR BAKER'S CATALOGUE
PO Box 876
Norwich, VT
05055-0876
800 827-6836

Sour salt, unhulled sesame seeds, Mexican vanilla, coarse salt, masa harina, baking equipment, thermometers

THE CMC COMPANY
PO Box 322
Avalon, NJ 08202
800 CMC-2780

Rick Bayless offers this specialty house if you are looking for: Avocado leaves, dried and canned chiles, masa harina, canned tomatillos, piloncillo, Mexican oregano, Mexican chocolate, anchiote paste, tortilla presses, molcajetes, comals and hot sauces.

ASIA MARKET
72 1/2 Mulberry St
New York, New York
212-962-2020

Asia Market is where Jean-Georges Vongerichten of Vong get his lemongrass and other ingredients, lemongrass is especially hard to find

URBANI TRUFFLES USA
29-24 40th Avenue
Long Island City, NY.
11101
718.392.5050 FAX
718.392.1704

Emeril Lagasse recommends Urbani Truffles USA, the largest distributor of all truffles in the United States. Current owners, Rosario and Andrew Safina, formed the company in 1983, purchasing the business from Paul Urbani, who introduced the truffle to the United States over 40 years ago

The YellowWeb Shopping Mall (http://www.yweb.com/shopping/mall09en.html) is one of the most unusual sources of foods on the Internet, with offerings such as Irish whiskey truffles and seafood soup. Listed on this home page are several different producers of specialty foods, all with links to their own home page. One of the caveats about using this international listing of foods is that it originates in Europe and so far, only serves countries such as Ireland, the United Kingdom, and Switzerland, but if you are in Switzerland and want a pizza, try http://www. pizzanet.ch/. Just so none of you North Americans feel left out, you can always visit the Web site for one of thousands of Pizza Hut restaurants (http://www.bigbook.com/showpage.cgi/3cc96c6c-0-0-0?page=listings_page&salesarea=NONE&company=pizza+hut&first=41).

Finally, if you live in or around Spokane, Washington, you'll find ingredients on the Food Specialties (http://www.spokane-areacvb.org/shop/food.htm) page. You can mail order from several of these establishments as well.

KITCHEN EQUIPMENT

There are vendors galore on the Internet, for everything from the most stylish of chef hats from Stylish Cooking (http://www.ny-works.com/rose/hat2.htm) to laundry equipment from Ateliers Reunnis Caddie (http://www.hospitalitynet.nl/vlist/caddie.htm).

The Vendor Showcase (http://www.hospitalitynet.nl/v/alpha.htm) lists more than six pages of vendors of supplies and equipment available from manufacturers and retailers all over the world. Included are dealers for dinnerware, uniforms, alcoholic beverages, cooking and warming equipment, consulting services, inventory systems, and food preparation equipment—almost anything you want from an international list of vendors. This home page is especially useful because you can sort by category or alphabetical listing, or even search.

Another equipment site, mostly industrial in its offerings, is Taylor Cooking Equipment (http://www.taylor-company.com/cook/cook.htm). Finally, for that black anodized perforated 12-inch pizza pan (named the Power Pan), you can check out Universal Power Systems at http://www.tecsolv.com/pizza/prices.htm.

Stylish Cooking Chef Hats

Remember, each Stylish Cooking hat is constructed with highly selected fabric for superior long wear. Inside of the hat is lined with a complimentary chosen fabric to suit the outer cap. The trim is cushioned with interfacing for a firm fit. The back of the hat is securely fastened with strong metal D-rings, to adjust to a head size of 20 1/2" to 27 1/2", comfortably.

MARSHMALLOW MERINGUE

The basic fluffy white on white chef hat, durable cotton twill cap, trim and lining. $30

PASSIONATE POINSETTIA

A robust cap full of blazing fiery red poinsettia flowers, surrounded by luscious evergreen leaves with a touch of gold. The trim is a traditional forest green and ultramarine blue plaid. $45

SPARKLING SPEARMINT

Glittering, sugary-like speckles on a frosted light green cap, enhanced with a cool mint green crisscross plaid trim. $45

STORES ONLINE

What you just read about are sites where ingredients and kitchen equipment are available on a more specialized basis. What you'll read about in this section are the actual online shops, some of which allow you to order right from your personal computer and have your purchase shipped to your home or office.

You can generally find places that have food and related goodies by searching in any of the mall sites on the Internet, and there are hundreds of those. Our search for shopping malls using the Excite search engine, turned up almost 500,000 hits, hundreds of which were direct! For example, the Mall Direct (`http://www.mdb1.com/shoplinks.htm`) Internet site lists the top 10 shopping sites on the Internet, such as the 21st Century mall (`http://www.21stcenturyplaza.com/`), Great Food Online (`http://www.greatfood.com/gfhome3.htm`), Flying Noodle Pasta Club (`http://www.flyingnoodle.com/`), Alaska Seafood Direct (`http://www.alaska.net/~asd/`), and The Indian River Fruit Company (`http://www.giftfruit.com/`). The Malls, Shopping, and Food site (`http://www.swcbc.com/SHOP.html`), has three pages of links to just that. Some browsing at these and other sites will reveal lots of food connections.

COMMERCIAL VENTURES ON THE ONLINE SERVICES

America Online, the Microsoft Network, and CompuServe Information Service all offer different types of online commercial offerings, mostly consisting of a listing of different vendors from which you can purchase food and food-related items.

One of the most comprehensive of these is Adventures in Food, found on CompuServe Information Service (**Find:** *Adventures In Food*). Adventures in Food is located in Hampton, New Hampshire, and unlike many other companies (on- and offline), they have the actual food they ship to you directly stored in their warehouse. You call, and they ship—so what you order is fresh. They offer an online selection including pastas made in their own kitchen and imported cheeses flown in from Europe. In addition, there are gift programs, recipes, and seasonal themes. This is a class operation that also has a site on the Web sponsored by Prodigy at `http://www.shopnet.prodigy.com/`.

The Gourmet Gift Net (**Find:** *Gourmet Gift Net*) on the Microsoft Network offers many different online shops carrying items raging from baskets to fish to spices and sauces. Several of these offer extensive collections of offerings such as Market Italian: Italian pesto and sauces, Italian chili oil, basil olive oil, and

truffle and porcini crème. Sweet Decadence offers Hall of Fame
Chocolate Roses, Pistachio Baklava, and Chocolations Edible
Pencils & Paper! If nothing else, these are fun places to visit.

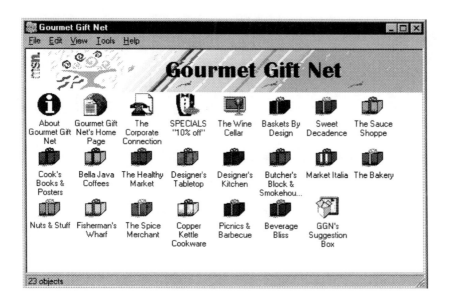

Finally, America Online offers The Marketplace (on the
Channels opening screen) where you can enter a contest, and of
course, buy food! Under Gourmet Gifts, you can find offerings
from Starbucks Coffee, Omaha Steaks, Hickory Farms, and
Godiva Chocolates. You can also search for catalogs from
specialty dealers such as the Chef's Catalog.

NUTRITION

The ICNN Nutrition Center

•

Diets

•

Low-fat Diets

It seems as if people are increasingly conscious of health issues, and probably at the top of the list is exercising and eating correctly. We can't help you with the exercise part here (although there is plenty on the line that can), but we can point you toward resources dealing with diet and health.

THE ICNN NUTRITION CENTER

The best online service place for information about nutrition is the Microsoft Network and the International Culinary & Nutrition Network Nutrition Center (or ICNN). You can go there using the **Find** command and the letters *ICNN*. This subforum contains a comprehensive selection of information covering offering such folders as Nutrition Questions & Answers, Personal Nutrition, Nutrition and Disease, Nutrients, Vitamins and Minerals, and Dietitians Online. How comprehensive is it? Within the Personal Nutrition area alone, you'll find

Pediatric Nutrition	General Nutrition
Adolescent Nutrition	Sports Nutrition
Women's Nutrition	Preventive Nutrition
Geriatric Nutrition	Vegetarian Nutrition
Nutrition and Pregnancy	Men's Nutrition

DIETS

Diets do not only mean dieting, they means eating a healthy, well-balanced diet. That's what Ask the Dietitian™ (http://www.hoptechno.com/rdindex.htm) is all about. As a part of Johns Hopkins University, Joanne Larsen (the dietitian you ask) offers extensive question and answer sessions on topics such as alcohol, bulimia, cancer, eating habits, fad diets, fast foods, potassium, teens, vegetables, vitamins, and at least 40 others. A click on any one of these leads to the entire manuscript of questions asked by real people and Dietitian Larsen's answers. This is very informative and a good starting point for anyone interested in issues of nutrition.

ASK THE DIETITIAN

(from http://www.hoptechno.com/cookhint.htm)

Q: Is there any harm in eating microwave foods daily? Do you have any information on the effects of a microwave?

A: Microwave cooking of food is not harmful, based on current research. In fact, microwaves preserve more of the vitamins and minerals in food because the food's exposure to heat and water is shorter than with conventional cooking methods.

Microwaves cause the water molecules in food to vibrate rapidly. It is this vibration that gives off heat, which cooks the food. What initially scared consumers about using microwaves was the warning on the door about radiation if the door was open. All microwaves have a safety mechanism that prevents you from operating the oven with the door open.

The only person who should not use a microwave oven is one who has a heart pacemaker implanted. The microwave could disrupt the electrical impulses produced by the pacemaker.

Fit and Healthy Lifestyles (http://odin.cc.pdx.edu/~psu03561/pm.htm) is also connected to the Hopkins efforts at encouraging people to maintain more healthy diets. This home page focuses on preventive medicine and discusses some of the most successful heart disease prevention diets that have become very popular and the authors who have made them such. The page offers links to the work of Dean Ornish, John McDougall, Gabe Merkin and the Merkin Report, and Terry Shintani.

You can also find helpful information from other Web sites dealing with diet and dieting. Among these are

- Overeaters Anonymous (http://www.hiwaay.net/recovery/), an organization of people working together to overcome compulsive eating.
- FITE (http://www.bright.net/~fite/), or Fat Is The Enemy, an advocacy group whose mission is to "turn the public spotlight on fat as a killer."
- The Duke Diet and Fitness Center (http://dmi-www.mc.duke.edu/dfc/home.html), the world-renowned center for nutrition, fitness, lifestyle counseling, and medical management.
- Dieting and Nutritional Information (gopher://gizmo.freenet.columbus.oh.us/11/healthservices/OSU%20Medical%20Center/Health%20Promotion%20and%20Disease%20Prevention%20Information/Nutrition%20and%20Diet) from the Ohio State Medical Center, which contains recipes and advice on healthy diets.

FOOD FACTS from CyberDiet at `http://www.cyberdiet.com/`

How to ruin a perfectly good potato!
I hope you're sitting down when you read this:

A medium baking potato is approximately 4 ounces, has 133 calories and 0.1 grams of fat. The commercially prepared bag of chips that comes with your lunch is ½ ounce, has 80 calories and 5 grams of fat.

If you took the medium potato and made it into chips, you would have 4 ounces of chips, (8 of those little bags), 640 calories and 40 grams of fat!

- CyberDiet (`http://www.cyberdiet.com/`), which contains information about almost everything concerning diet and health including what type of aerobic exercise to do, facts on foods, and testimonials (and some selling as well!).
- Finally, the American Heart Association (`http://www.amhrt.org/pubs/ahadiet.html`) offers An Eating Plan for Healthy Americans. It's 400K in size and will take a few minutes to download from their Web site (in QuarkXpress format), but is probably a good thing to look at if you are interested in a low-fat, low-cholesterol diet.

LOW-FAT DIETS

The Internet, in many ways, reflects what our every day lives are about. It's no surprise to find that most of the diet-related information on the Internet has to do with low-fat diets, ranging from newsletters to recipes.

The best place to start is Julie's Low & Fat Free Resource List (`http://www.eskimo.com/~baubo/lowfat.html`), which is full of home pages that include recipes, shops specializing in low-fat products, specific foods, herbs, and, of course, many of the fun pages you find throughout this book. More recipes can be found at Low-Fat, High-Flavor Dining (`http://www.bpe.com/food/recipes/pappas/`), including An Italian Style Feast, A Provençal Dinner with Friends, and a Seafood Supper from Portugal.

Low-Fat Living (`http://www.xe.net/lowfat/editor.htm`) from the home page (`http://www.xe.net/lowfat/`) has as its mandate to help the average person achieve a low-fat lifestyle. Jane Sarjeant, the editor of *Low-Fat Living*, provides ideas, recipes, and tips and tricks for modifying a potentially unhealthy lifestyle without eliminating your favorite foods.

TIP

From the *Low-Fat Living* Home Page (`http://www.xe.net/lowfat/tips/tip_0001.htm`)

Replace some of the whole eggs called for with 2 egg whites. Each egg replaced with 2 egg whites will save 5 grams of fat. It's usually a good idea to keep at least 1 or 2 whole eggs to maintain the correct taste and consistency. For example, replace 3 whole eggs with 1 whole egg and 4 egg whites—you'll save 10 grams of fat.

TALKING KITCHEN TALK

UseNet Groups

•

Talk on the Internet

Anyone who is serious about cooking, whether for a Saturday night with good friends or in a four-star restaurant, knows the importance of being able to share ideas with others. There are some wonderful sources for interacting with great chefs as well as just plain cooks on the Internet, and we'll show you these here. In general, the big online services don't offer any significant opportunity to chat about food, but they all do have general chat rooms where you can meet people and suggest they talk about food.

The real treasures are found in Usenet groups, where participants create and follow a thread of discussion by reading other contributions and then contributing their own. We talked about how to use newsgroups earlier. Here's a rundown of some of the most active ones.

USENET GROUPS

In the first chapter, "Getting Started Online," we talked about newsgroups much as if they were like bulletin boards. You can post a message in response to someone else's or start your own thread of conversation about food. Where can you do this? Here's a listing of some of the major news groups associated with food. Keep in mind how quickly the contents of the Internet are changing, so what you see here today may not be here tomorrow, but there will surely be something better to replace it.

alt.coookies.yum.yum.yum	rec.food.equipment
alt.food.cooking	rec.food.historic
alt.food.fast-food	rec.food.marketplace
alt.restaurants	rec.food.preserving
rec.food.baking	rec.food.recipes
rec.food.chocolate	rec.food.sourdough
rec.food.cooking	rec.food.veg.cooking
rec.food.drink.beer	

For example, remember the recipe in "Chocolate" for Mrs. Fields' cookies? Here's a peek at one of the contributions to the rec.food.chocolate newsgroup that talks about another urban legend regarding Neiman-Marcus cookies. The posted message and recipe are on the next page. Remember that newsgroups are not real time. You cannot talk directly with people. Rather, you leave your contribution and come back later to read what other people have to say. If you want to get started using newsgroups and doing food things, your Internet browser has a function that allows you to read news. Review what we covered earlier for more information.

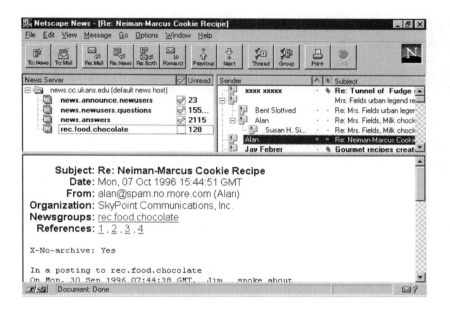

TALK ON THE INTERNET

On the Internet, StarChefs (http://www.starchefs.com/ chefscorner.html) has a nice little feature titled Dear StarChefs, where you can make contact with any of the chefs that are featured in the current issue. This is not a place for questions about the Web site, but rather an opportunity for you to ask questions about recipes, offer your own ideas, and learn from some of the best.

COOKIE RECIPE FOR SALE

Here's a real live story that has made its way around the net and usually involves Mrs. Fields or Neiman-Marcus cookies.

My daughter & I had just finished a salad at Neiman-Marcus Cafe in Dallas & decided to have a small dessert. Because both of us are such cookie lovers, we decided to try the "Neiman-Marcus Cookie." It was so excellent that I asked if they would give me the recipe and the waitress said with a small frown, "I'm afraid not." Well, I said, would you let me buy the recipe?

With a cute smile, she said, "Yes." I asked how much, and she responded, "Only two fifty, it's a great deal!" I said with approval, just add it to my tab. Thirty days later, I received my VISA statement from Neiman-Marcus and it was $285.00. I looked again and I remembered I had only spent $9.95 for two salads and about $20.00 for a scarf. As I glanced at the bottom of the statement, it said, "Cookie Recipe—$250.00." That's outrageous!! I called Neiman's Accounting Dept. and told them the waitress said it was "two-fifty," which clearly does not mean "two hundred and fifty dollars" by any *POSSIBLE* interpretation of the phrase. Neiman-Marcus refused to budge. They would not refund my money, because according to them, "What the waitress told you is not our problem. You have already seen the recipe—we absolutely will not refund your money at this point." I explained to her the criminal statutes which govern fraud in Texas, I threatened to refer them to the Better Business Bureau and the State's Attorney General for engaging in fraud. I was basically told, "Do what you want, we don't give a crap, and we're not refunding your money." I waited, thinking of how I could get even, or even try and get any of my money back.

I just said, "Okay, you folks got my $250, and now I'm going to have $250.00 worth of fun." I told her that I was going to see to it that every cookie lover in the United States with an e-mail account has a $250.00 cookie recipe from Neiman-Marcus…for free. She replied, "I wish you wouldn't do this." she said, "Well, you should have thought of that before you ripped me off, and slammed down the phone on her.

So, here it is!!! Please, please, please pass it on to everyone you can possibly think of. I paid $250 for this…. I don't want Neiman-Marcus to *ever* get another penny off of this recipe….

2 cups butter	1 tsp salt
4 cups flour	1-8 oz Hershey Bar (grated)
2 tsp soda	4 eggs
2 cups sugar	2 tsp baking powder
5 cups blended oatmeal*	3 cups chopped nuts (your choice)
24 oz chocolate chips	2 tsp vanilla
2 cups brown sugar	

*Measure oatmeal and blend in a blender to a fine powder. Cream the butter and both sugars. Add eggs and vanilla; mix together with flour, oatmeal, salt, baking powder, and soda. Add chocolate chips, Hershey Bar and nuts. Roll into balls and place two inches apart on a cookie sheet. Bake for 10 minutes at 375 degrees. Makes 112 cookies. Have fun!!!

This is *not* a joke—this is a true story.

COOKBOOKS AND ELECTRONIC MAGAZINES

Information about Cookbooks

•

Electronic Magazines, or E-zines

Did you know that more than 60,000 new titles are published each year in the United States alone and a significant number of these (more than 10%) are cookbooks? And what good epicure (online or otherwise) doesn't have at least one or two cookbooks to call his or her own? Ones that have dog-eared pages, where you have memorized the page on which the cold spicy chicken or waffle recipe is located?

You won't find the entire text of many cookbooks online, but you will find plenty of information on cookbooks in general. The Internet especially offers a way for you to find the book you need and even allows you to order it.

INFORMATION ABOUT COOKBOOKS

If you're looking for a particular book and know the title or author, try the most general Internet resource first—namely, Amazon Books (`http://www.amazon.com`), where you can search for a title from over a million on file. For example, let's see what a search on the keyword cookbooks turns up—well, thousands of titles and even too many for them to display. You can spend time browsing through those titles, or you can be a little more specific. A search for books on Greek food turns up 9 titles, and a search for books on high-fiber cooking turns up 5 titles. Surely you could find one among these that you could use if you were a looking for a book in a particular area.

A simple search using AltaVista for cooks turns up 7,000 hits, including companies such as General Publishing at `http://www.fundraising-cookbooks.com/`, which helps create cookbooks for organizations such as churches and synagogues; a source of rare cookbooks (`http://www.eden.com/~bgg/cookbks.html`) from The Book Garden Gallery; cookbooks from manufacturers of food such as Campbell's Soups at `http://www.campbellsoups.com/!!r05wa2M7dr05wa2M7d/books/Welcome2.html`; and cookbooks from retailers such as Vintage Direct at `http://www.sofcom.com.au/Nicks/Cookbooks.html`. For more about cookbooks, be sure to check out the giant Yahoo page on cookbooks at `http://gnn.yahoo.com/gnn/Entertainment/Food_and_Eating/Recipes/Cookbooks`.

PERSONALITY: CHEFS ON THE NET

Don Zajaz knows two things: You have to have a passion for what you do and you have to stay ahead of the curve. He loves being the executive chef at Floosmoor Country Club, 35 miles south of Chicago. He's also never lost sight of advice his teachers gave him to look to the future. That's why he's an active member of several e-mail groups and newsgroups such as ChefNet. Chefs are a tightly knit group and are willing to help one another with everything from recipes to managing business. When one of Don's chef friends asked him about using ostrich meat as a low-fat alternative, he got on the Internet and was rewarded with pages of information including recipes and tips on how to cook this meat, relatively new to the United States, as well as what to cook with it. For Don, the online information about food is here to stay.

ELECTRONIC MAGAZINES (E-ZINES)

E-zines are electronic magazines or the counterpart of the print one you can hold in your hands. We found five e-zines on the Internet. Here's a brief description of each along with the URL so you can explore by yourself.

The electronic *Gourmet Guide* (eGG) (http://www.foodwine. com), shown on the following page, is the Internet's first food and cooking magazine (1994), and features interviews with chefs and other food industry professionals, feature articles, food news, cooking tips, new recipes, regular columnists, the Global Gourmet, and the Gourmet Guess food quiz.

The *Gourmet Connection eMagazine* (http://www.norwich.net/ gourmet/link1.htm) Is an award-winning e-zine that features monthly articles and recipes (with nutritional info), The Diabetic Gourmet, Culinary/Health Trivia, Product Reviews, and Pro's Corner.

Gourmet Fare (http://www.ceo-online.com/gourmet) is a print and electronic food and entertainment magazine with articles of interest for all food lovers. Departments include Health, Travel, Kids in the Kitchen, Cookbooks, Wine, Beverages, EuroGourmet, and much more.

The *Internet Epicurean* (http://www.epicurean.com) is an e-zine of resources for the gourmet that contains articles on food and drink, features menus, an has an interactive Recipe Exchange, Recipe Archives, a Chef's forum, a Cook's Calculator, and the Chef's Shop.

American Cake Decorating (http://www.cakemag.com) is the only full-featured magazine dedicated to the art of cake decorating—cakes, ideas, hints, tips, techniques, personalities, and more.

foodwine.com

Welcome to foodwine.com. Please be sure to **bookmark this page** rather than dated articles.

Updated Daily

Today's FoodDay

Updated Weekly

Foodscape Contents

   Net Food Digest
   eGG-Roll Excerpts
   Back of the House
   Food, Family & Fun
   Lisa Ekus Presents...

more foodwine

American Wine on the Web

The Blue Directory of
Food and Beverage Sites

The eGGbasket Gourmet
Store

Message Boards

The eGG Archives

Cooking Calculator

The eGG on AOL

Opportunities On the eGG

Staff

Kudos

Viewing Tips

 electronic Gourmet Guide

The eGG: Issue 27 - November 1996

What's New This Month

Features

Thanksgiving No-Brainer by Kate Heyho

Pheasants and Other Turkey Alternatives
John Manikowski

Top Turkey Secrets from "Jimmy Schmid
Cooking Class"

Columns

Just Good Food...for Thought by John Ry

Culinary Sleuth by Lynn Kerrigan

eGGsalad by Prof. Steve Holzinger

Global Gourmet Cookbook

The Rest

Gourmet Guess Food Trivia Game
sponsored by Black & Decker

Quick Tip

Did You Know

Toasts & Quotes

James Beard Calendar

Letters to the Editor

Index of This Issue's Recipes

Search the eGG

RESTAURANT REVIEWS

Restaurant Reviews on America Online

•

Restaurant Reviews on CompuServe

•

Restaurant Reviews on Microsoft Network

•

Restaurant Reviews on the Internet

The best way to find a great place to eat is to ask another food lover. The second best way might be to consult one of the thousands of food reviews available on line.

Whether you're considering restaurants in New York, Los Angeles, Paris, Hong King, or even down the block, you can find out online what the experts are saying about them. You can discover the best Italian restaurant in Cincinnati, the best Thai food in Boston, and even the name of the chef preparing the food. With the Internet at your fingertips, "Where do you want to eat?" takes on a whole new meaning.

RECIPES ON AMERICA ONLINE

America Online offers two places to go for locating restaurant reviews in your quest for that great meal out of the house. The first and most useful source for information on eating out on America Online is the comprehensive Zagat guides (keyword: *Zagat*), offering an extensive set of reviews of restaurants nationwide.

Zagat reviews are available for 30 major metropolitan areas: Atlanta; Atlantic City; Baltimore; Boston; Chicago; Cincinnati; Cleveland; Columbus; Dallas; Denver; Honolulu; Houston; Kansas City; Los Angeles; Miami; New Orleans; New York; Orange County, Calif.; Orlando; Palm Beach; Philadelphia; Phoenix-Scottsdale; Portland; Salt Lake City; San Diego; San Francisco; Santa Fe; Seattle; St. Louis; and Washington, D.C.

What's most useful about the Zagat reviews is that each review rates the restaurant in three categories—food, decor, and service—on a 30-point scale. Zero to nine points is poor to fair, 10 to 19 points is good to very good, 20 to 25 is very good to excellent, and 25 to 30 points is extraordinary to fabulous. The reviews also list a fourth number, which is the cost of a typical dinner for one person with one alcoholic drink and tip. Lunches generally are about 25% less. For example, in Seattle, Adriatica serves Mediterranean food with a flair and gets scores of 25 for food, 23 for decor, and 23 for service, with the average cost of a meal being $30.

Within the Zagat reviews, you can search for restaurants in a number of ways. You can search by restaurant name, type of food, ranking, or price, or you can seek only those listed as top bargains. No matter how you search, you'll find hundreds of restaurant reviews for these metropolitan areas.

The second place to go for reviews is the *Washingtonian* magazine restaurant database (keyword: *Washingtonian*) which you can search by neighborhood, price, and cuisine, but only one factor at a time. One of the wonderful things about the District of Columbia and surrounding areas is that there are so many foreign diplomats, there are many ethnic restaurants that try to meet their tastes.

We searched by location in the Alexandria, Virginia area and found 26 reviews of restaurants. Each review contains the address, phone number, approximate price, and what credit cards are accepted. The Washingtonian site also lists the 100 best bargains and the 100 very best restaurants throughout this metropolitan area.

RECIPES ON COMPUSERVE

The Dining Out library (in the Cooks forum) is the place to start on CompuServe for information about restaurants and restaurant reviews. It's organized by content such as Best Restaurants in Belgium or Dining in Phoenix or Memories of a Cuban Kitchen. As with any other forum on CompuServe, you can contribute your own thoughts and ideas as well as read those of others. In some ways, this free flow of information can give a more honest assessment of a restaurant's offerings than a commercial service such as Zagat.

The Dining On Us Club is a commercial area on CompuServe which offers a parallel service to that offered by companies that sell coupon books. After joining, you can get discounts such as 2 for 1 at selected restaurants, free movie tickets, and other types of discounts.

RESTAURANTS ON THE MICROSOFT NETWORK

The Microsoft Network offers reviews of individual restaurants, but no general location for finding restaurants or groups of reviews.

THE 10 VERY BEST SEAFOOD RESTAURANTS IN WASHINGTON, D.C.

(compliments of America Online)

Tara Thai
China Inn
Union Street Public House
Benjarong
Good Fortune
Seven Seas
Tachibana
Tako Grill
Kinkheads
Crescent City

RESTAURANT REVIEWS ON THE INTERNET

The easiest way to find a review of a restaurant on the Internet is to use one of the many available search engines and enter the location or type of cuisine and the location. In general, you'll find three categories of restaurant reviews on the Internet—those published as part of online activities by newspapers, search tools, and general reviews by food organizations; commercial home pages; and home pages published by individuals—and just about everything else.

REVIEWS IN ONLINE NEWSPAPERS

There are hundreds of newspapers that offer reviews, most of them concentrating on their own geographical location and ranging in quality from simple text presentations to sophisticated search tools. If you are looking for a restaurant review in a local area, it's best to use one of the search engines discussed earlier such as AltaVista and enter search words such as "restaurants in kansas city." You'll find all you need to get started. For example, a search for restaurants in Bloomington, Indiana, resulted in a sizeable list of restaurants (`http://www.cs.indiana.edu/csgsa/ outreach/restrev/dir.html`), all with links to their own home page.

The most attractive and informative of these online newspaper reviewers is from the *Kentucky Herald-Leader* (`http://www.kentuckyconnect.com/heraldleader/restaurants/index.htm`) with an alphabetical listing of restaurants surrounding the University of Kentucky.

One of the easiest and most sophisticated of the newspaper-sponsored reviews is offered by the Meriden, Connecticut–based *Record-Journal* in their Dining Out guide (`http://www.record-journal.com/rest/restndx.htm`). You select the geographical area around Meriden and Dining Out produces a list of restaurants with accompanied reviews from which you can select.

Three newspapers that offer online reviews of restaurants in their local area are *The Chicago Tribune* (`http://www.chicago.tribune.com/print/goodeat/current/goodeat.html`), *The Palo Alto Weekly* (`http://www.service.com/PAW/thisweek/restaurants/1996_Sep_18.mini_reviews.html`), *The Times of Calumet*

(`http://www.calunet.com/calunet/restaurants/restaurants.html`)
—yes, it really is spelled calu**ne**t in the URL), and *The Northwest Portland Newspaper* (`http://elaine-1.teleport.com/~neighbor/restrv01.html`). Your local newspaper might very well do the same. Call them and find out if they have a URL and what it is. We selected these online examples because they seem to be fairly thorough in their reviews and provide a good example of how a restaurant should be evaluated.

RESTAURANT REVIEW SEARCH ENGINES

Search engines are always fun to use. You simply enter the words that describe location, type, and price of the restaurant, click on Search or Find, and the search tool does the rest.

The biggest and best is the Zagat Dine home page (`http://pathfinder.com/Travel/Zagat/Dine/index.html`), shown on the following page, where you click on the city of choice, such as Miami, and then browse and search alphabetically, by cuisine, by food ranking, by popularity, or by top bargains. You read earlier how Zagat uses a fairly objective system for rating food, decor, and service. This is a good starting point should you be traveling to any of the 30 areas the guide covers.

Cyber-Dine (`http://www.cyber-view.com/cyber/state.html`) offers search capabilities for all 50 states, then by cuisine type, name of restaurant, price range, and keyword. If we select **Kansas** and then enter "Kansas City" as the city of interest and "American" in the Restaurant Name space, we'll find 10 different restaurants, including the American Restaurant whose phone number was needed to make a reservation.

If you live in New Jersey, New Jersey Online Eats (`http://www.nj.com/arts/eats/rest2.html`) is terrific. It covers all of New Jersey and selects by type of food, price range, or county, or you can type in a town or a specific restaurant to see if it's reviewed. Want a moderately priced restaurant anywhere in Essex County (bordering New York City)? Eats found eight restaurants from which to select. You'll also find links on this home page to the restaurant reviews in *The Newark Star-Ledger* and *Philadelphia Inquirer* newspapers.

In the Southern New Jersey and Philadelphia area, you can also use the Interactive Restaurant Reviews search tool (http://www.delcom.com/IRR/Feedback.html), where you can enter your own review or browse through different geographic locations (such as Wilmington, Delaware, or Atlantic City, New Jersey) and also examine reviews entered during the last few days or the last week.

GENERAL REVIEWS

By far the most ambitious category, these home pages come in all levels of sophistication and usually are confined to a small or large geographical area. Some, however, are unique, such as Bring Me My Dinner (http://www.townline.com/bmmd/bmmdcity.htm), which offers an extensive listing of restaurants that deliver in the

Greenwich, Stamford, Fairfield, Weston, and adjacent areas in Connecticut. For example, if you live in Darien and want to know about what's at Kathleen's and delivery hours, you're just a click away from that information. Actually, the Pan Fried Maryland Crab Cakes with Creoleaise and Endive Salad for $8 sounds quite appetizing. It sure saves trying to find all those carryout menus.

CusineNet (http://www.cuisinenet.com/), on the following page, is a new and ambitious entry into the food online field and includes an interesting area of restaurant reviews. Through Restaurant Central (http://www.cuisinenet.com/restaurant/index.html), CuisineNet provides descriptions, menus, and reviews for thousands of restaurants based on location, cuisine type, price, and even child friendliness (it's about time!). They only review restaurants in five cities so far (New York, Chicago, Seattle, Boston, and San Francisco), but the information is comprehensive. They even tell you what to wear and where to park! Best of all, this is really a fun site to visit.

Grapevine (http://www.dinersgrapevine.com/) bills itself as "the premiere on-line dining guide," and if it is not the best, it certainly is the most comprehensive—with over 8,000 restaurants listed. As with other home pages like this one, you can search for a variety of different restaurants, not only in the United States, but in all over the world including Europe, the Caribbean, South America, Australia, and more. You search on country, state, city, zip code, atmosphere (dim lights), special features (artwork or the availability of online computers), and entertainment, including belly dancing and singing waiters. You enter the price (up to $1,000), and then, "When it's time to dine, pick from the vine" (or so the page reads).

Less focused, but just full of information about restaurants is the Yahoo (the search engine) page (http://www.yahoo.com/Business_and_Economy/Companies/Restaurants/Directories/), which lists topic after topic dealing with restaurants including 10 commercial Web sites such as dineAmerica (http://www.dineamerica.com/), Emeal Restaurant Listings (http://www.emeal.com/), and WebMenu (http://www.webmenu.com/). There's a lot of advertising on these home pages but also tons of links to other locations that will give you good information on restaurants throughout the country. Yahoo (http://www.yahoo.com/Entertainment/Food_and_Eating/Restaurants/Regional_Reviews/) also offers reviews of restaurants by regional area.

I'm Frederick, your concierge, here to introduce you to **CuisineNet**, the Web's ever-expanding dining guide and food resource.

Visit Restaurant Central, the best place to window shop for restaurants. From dress codes to phone numbers, Restaurant Central gathers together all the information you need to find out how a place feels from wherever you sit. Plus, here's where you can be the critic. Rate a restaurant and tell the world all about that meal!

Stop in at the CuisineNet Cafe for lively reports from and engaging discussions about the world of food. Our columns and forums make it the perfect place to whet your appetite.

Explore the Diner's Digest when you're wondering about coconut milk (is it the juice inside?) or when you want to take a virtual tour of the world of food. From Thailand to Texas, the Diner's Digest takes you there.

Try the Market when you're ready to shop for the kitchen. Ben, our virtual shopkeeper, is still stocking up, so keep checking back.

And right now, please sign our **Guest Book**!

Restaurant Central

Visit Restaurant Central and explore your dining choices in New York City. Check out Boston, San Francisco, Chicago, and Seattle. Chloe, our virtual critic, is busy building up our databases for these cities and for the rest of the country.

The CuisineNet Poll

Want something to eat with that drink? Would you choose:

☐ Fried Calamari

☐ Small Pizza

Check the Latest Results

At The Cafe

You Gonna Eat That?
by Marjorie Ingall
The Cocktail Party: A Trend is Dead

THE TABLE
Join our Forums! This week's topics:
The Martini, what is it we're all happily resurrecting?

In The Market

LAMALLE KITCHENWARE
Check out Lamalle Kitchenware's online store.

CuisineNet Highlights

Here's what they're saying! CuisineNet Visitors are making their voice heard!

CuisineNet Top Spots on the web
CuisineNet Top Spots on the Web

For more great food on the Web, check out the electronic Gourmet Guide!

European Mirror site

R I C H A R D S

RESTAURANT RANKING

"All About The Finest Restaurants In The World"

About RRR	The Best Meal In The World	Awards & Comments
Links to Others	Search	email RRR

Ranking	Restaurant name	Chef	Link	MICHELIN	GAULT&MILLAU
1	Les Crayeres, Reims, France	Gerard Boyer	❀	★ ★ ★	17/20
2	Troisgros, Roanne, France	Michel Troisgros	❀	★ ★ ★	19/20
3	Pic, Valence, France	Alain Pic	❀	♟♟♟ ★ ★	17/20
4	Alain Chapel, Mionnay, France	Philippe Jousse	❀	★ ★	18/20
5	Paul Bocuse, Collonges-au-mont d'or (Lyon), France	Paul Bocuse	ℬ	♟♟♟♟♟ ★ ★ ★	17/20
6	La côte Saint Jaques, Joigny, France	Michel Lorain	❀	★ ★ ★	18/20
7	Le Moulin de Mougins, Mougins, France	Roger Vergé	❀	♟♟♟♟ ★ ★	17/20
8	Le Louis XV, Monaco	Alain Ducasse	No	♟♟♟♟♟ ★ ★ ★	19/20
9	L'Abbaye st. Michel, Tonnere, France	Daniel et Christophe Cusac	❀	★ ★	16/20
10	Auberge du Lion D'or, Cologny (Genève), Suisse	-	No	★ ★	15/20
11	Lameloise, Chagny, France	Jaques Lameloise	❀	★ ★ ★	17/20
12	Lucas Carton, Paris	Alain Senderens	No	♟♟♟♟♟♟ ★ ★ ★	18
13	Enoteca Pinchiorri, Florence, Italy	Annie Féolde	❀	★ ★	None
14	Chez Bruno, Lorgues, France	Clément Bruno	No	♟♟♟ ★	16/20
15	Paul & Norbert, Stockholm, Sweden	Norbert Lang	No	★	None
16	Le Cagnard, Cagnes sur mer, France		❀	★	16
17	Franska matsalen (Grand Hôtel), Stockholm, Sweden	Roland Persson	No	♟♟♟♟	None
18	Le Château de Courcelles, Courcelles-sur-Vesle, France	-	❀	♟♟♟	14/20
19	Le Manoir, Fontenay Tresigny, France		❀	♟♟	14/20
20	Château de Rochegude, Rochegude, France	-	❀	♟♟♟	None
21	Hostellerie des Clos, Chablis, France	Michel Vignaud	No	♟♟ ♟♟ ★	16/20

Shown on the previous page is Richards Restaurant Ranking (http://www.lagerling.se/rest.html), which lists some of the world's best restaurants. Clicking on any restaurant name reveals pictures, history, and menus—how civilized. You'll also find the ratings found in the Michelin and Gault & Millau guides, both European standards.

More regional reviews can be found in the Natural Resource Directory (http://www.itlnet.com/natural/nrd/sect3c.html) focusing on California restaurants in a 10-page home page. The Gourmet Web (http://www.gourmetweb.com/search.html) offers reviews for restaurants in the New Jersey/Philadelphia area, and there's a very nice list of full-size restaurant reviews at http://www.projo.com/horizons/postcards/review.htm for eateries in Rhode Island, each one with a link to the restaurant so that you can find out more.

COOKING SCHOOLS AND CLASSES

Start Here

•

Professional Schools

•

Nonprofessional Schools

•

Lists of Schools and Classes

Whether you're considering a career change to become that sous-chef you always wanted to be or are just looking for a 2-week baking course in Southern Italy, you can find hundreds of options for cooking schools and classes on the Internet. Most of what you will find is divided into two groups: professional and nonprofessional or avocational instruction. The distinction between the two is mostly in the amount of time the program or class lasts. For example, the well-known French Culinary Institute has 9- and 16-month courses, whereas the Villa Table in Chianti, Italy (more for nonprofessionals), offers 1-week courses.

START HERE

Whether you are looking for professional or nonprofessional cooking classes and schools, the ShawGuides (`http://www.shawguides.com/shacooking.html`) database allows you to define the type of program (career, nonvocational, vacation), the state (in the United States), and the location (USA or All). Click on the Search button and you'll be given a selection of sites that meet the criteria you defined.

ShawGuides
The Guide to Cooking Schools

Search the ShawGuides Database

Select a program: | Career Programs |

Select a state: | National/International |

Select a country: | All |

[Search] [Reset]

Home

Then move on to the Kitchen Link's section on Cooking Schools/Institutes (`http://www.kitchenlink.com/ref.html#Cooking Schools/Institutes`), which lists more than 20 schools as links to the school's home page, including many that are discussed later in this chapter.

PROFESSIONAL SCHOOLS

These are some of the schools you might want to consider if you have plans to become a professional in the culinary field. An excellent starting point is StarChefs (`http://www.starchefs.com/helpwanted.html`), which provides information on culinary schools and culinary organizations, and help wanted ads for culinary professionals. Many of the schools that are mentioned on the StarChefs home page are discussed in the paragraphs that follow, but this is a good place to start looking for what might interest you. StarChefs offers a terrific help-wanted section where you can respond to ads or place your own.

THE FRENCH CULINARY INSTITUTE

(`http://plaza.interport.net/fci/fci.html`)

Speaking of the French Culinary Institute, if you have the time (6- or 9-month programs), want to learn the art of French cooking in the United States, and are very serious about this undertaking, you should consider this as a stop. Founded in 1984 by Dorothy Cann Hamilton, it has among its faculty some of the best known Chefs in the business, and as a slogan, *Qualité, Discipline, Réalité.*

As with many culinary schools, the French Culinary Institute sponsors a restaurant where students apply their skills. You can get a five-course price-fixed lunch ($15.99) or dinner ($22), and menus are mouth watering. At these prices and this quality, it's a good idea to get a reservation [(212) 219-3300]. After four levels of training, and 600 hours, the graduates from the French Culinary Institute move on to some of the finest restaurants in America.

Want a wonderful, yet inexpensive, five-course meal in New York City? Try the French Culinary Institute's offerings.
Here's the 5-day menu from a recent week.

Monday
Cream of Mushroom Soup
Salad Provençale
Poached Trout with Butter Sauce
Pork Chops with Mushroom Duxelles
Crème Brulée
Peach Tart

Tuesday
Vegetable Soup
Salmon Cakes with Haricots Verts
Chicken Curry with Wild Rice
Blueberry Tart with Cassis Sorbet
Raspberry Puff Pastry Tart

Wednesday
Lemon Soup with Mint and Couscous
Beef Carpaccio
Fish Stew with Aioli
Sauteed Kidneys with Mustard
Phyllo with Chocolate and Raspberries
Exotic Fruit Soup with Vanilla Ice Cream

Thursday
Consommé
Tomato Tart
Salmon with Summer Vegetables
Grilled Duck with a Citrus Sauce and Potatoes
Fig Tart with Honey Sauce
Cherry Crêpe

Friday
Gazpacho
Stuffed Vegetables
Sea Scallops with a Ginger Sauce
Filet of Beef with Braised Endive
Fruit Cake
Strawberry Puff Pastry Tart

Saturday (same as Friday)

THE CULINARY INSTITUTE OF AMERICA

(http://www.thomson.com/partners/cia/default.html)

The best-known culinary institute in America (and in many other parts of the world as well) is the Culinary Institute of America, with schools located in Hyde Park, New York, and Napa Valley, California. CIA by the Numbers (a Web page entry) tells you why: 11 American Culinary Federation-certified master chefs are on the faculty along with some 120 other faculty and staff, a language lab with 30 workstations, a computer lab with more than 80 workstations, 36 professionally equipped kitchens and bakeshops, and over 4,000 meals prepared each day, served by students.

The CIA's home page, shown on the following page, is full of information including a detailed description of the curriculum, career opportunities, information about the four on-campus restaurants (including the American Bounty, the Escoffier Restaurant, the Catrina De Medici Dining Room, and the St. Andrew's Café), information about admissions and financial matters, and a message from the president. You can start your CIA career one of 16 times throughout the year. Plan on spending about $15,000 to cover your tuition and living costs—not a small amount, but what you receive is well worth it.

LE CORDON BLEU

(http://sunsite.unc.edu/expo/restaurant/history.html)

The CIA might have one of the best programs available, but Le Cordon Bleu has the fine patina of old age—going strong since 1896, when it started in Paris' Palais Hotel. Today, the school offers classes in France, England, Japan, and Canada. Their home page is not very informative, but if you're after prestige, this is the place to consider.

THE CULINARY INSTITUTE OF AMERICA

433 Albany Post Road
Hyde Park, New York 12538-1499
914-452-9600

For comments and/or suggestions, contact the CIA Webmaster.

- A Message from the President
- CIA by the Numbers UPDATED
- Learn from the Very Best UPDATED
- Degree Options UPDATED
- Career Exploration
- How to Apply NEW *View/print an application form!*
- Financial Information UPDATED
- Continuing Education (Hyde Park, NY)
- The Culinary Institute of America at Greystone (Napa Valley, CA)
- Video Sales NEW *View/print order forms!*
- Restaurant Information UPDATED *New sample menus!*
- Campus Map (Hyde Park, NY) NEW
- Travel Directions (Hyde Park, NY)
- 50th Anniversary Year Calendar of Events
- PBS Television Series "Cooking Secrets of the CIA"

PENNSYLVANIA CULINARY (http://www.pacul.com/)

Pennsylvania Culinary is the third largest culinary institute in the United States with over 1,100 students. Their home page offers a weekly recipe (Chiffon Cake the week we checked) as well as a recipe archives for searching back for previous recipes. You can also enter to win a Pennsylvania Culinary t-shirt. Many of the recipes found in the archives are prepared and served by students at the school's restaurant, Brendan's. It serves lunch and you usually need a reservation to be sure you can get in. With a Bronze Chicken Breast for $5.25 and the dessert of the day at $1.25, it's no wonder it's crowded.

NEW ENGLAND CULINARY INSTITUTE

(http://www.neculinary.com/neci/welcome.htm)

The NECI is another outstanding professional school, but it also offers shorter courses such as a 3-day bread-making program and a weekend course for chocolate dessert lovers. Both of these are open to other than full-time students and supplement the 2-year Associate's degree, the 3-year Bachelor's degree, and the 1-year certificate in basic food preparation. You can even apply for admission online.

PROFESSIONAL COOKING SCHOOLS

(http://www.bpe.com/food/reference/cookingschools/pro.html)

If you're not interested in traveling to any one of the schools just mentioned, then how about staying closer to home? Here you can find schools in Arizona, California, Colorado, Florida, Illinois, and 12 other states. Each school is accompanied by a description of what types of programs are available and instructions for getting in touch. You'll find some interesting schools here as well as additional information on some of those featured earlier.

PROFESSIONAL BARTENDING SCHOOL

(http://www.netpage1.com/pbs/course.html)

Finally, if you want to skip the food and move right to the drinks, this 2-week (40-hour) course consists of day or evening classes and even teaches you when to offer coffee to a patron when closing time is already past. Located in Austin, Texas, the school offers job placement and a hands-on curriculum where classes are taught (where else?) at the bar.

NONPROFESSIONAL SCHOOLS

Now the weekend warrior chef takes over. You'll find here a mix of opportunities, from the local food shop at the mall offering a 1-day class in baking bread to professional schools (like those mentioned above), offering classes to nonprofessionals who have limited time for such activities. To begin with, even if they're not online, try your local community or junior college. They almost invariably offer some type of culinary training, often offering both an extended Associate's degree and evening and shortened classes.

THE NORTHERN CALIFORNIA CENTER FOR THE CULINARY ARTS

(http://www.omix.com/nccca/)

Here's an offer that would be hard to resist. The NCCCA, which was started in the fall of 1991, offers small cooking classes that are conducted in the restaurant kitchens of local, regional, and world-renowned chefs. You actually cook in the restaurant. This is one of the schools that has something for cooks at all levels of proficiency and welcomes any and everyone for their classes in one of 18 venues.

THE MOVING COOKING SCHOOL

http://www.omix.com/nccca/

The NCCCA offers its classes through the facilities of restaurants and the chefs who staff them. Take a look at some of these recent offerings from their home page.

Kuleto's Trattoria—Burlingame, California

This fabulous Italian-style trattoria in Burlingame is headed by Chef Jackie Watson. The highly popular restaurant is known for its unique Italian style, incorporating tremendous intensity of flavors along with the best regional items available. Chef Jackie Watson creates for you what many restaurant critics call "the best trattoria and Italian food south of San Francisco."

Tourelle—Lafayette, California

Come join us for a sensational class at one of the culinary hot spots of the East Bay. Located in Lafayette, this gorgeous restaurant is under the vigilant guidance of Chef Stephen Silva. Beautiful food, equal in both flavor and diversity, awaits you at this ever-popular restaurant.

COOKING SCHOOLS: JUST PLAIN FUN

(http://www.bpe.com/food/reference/cookingschools/cont.html)

Earlier in this chapter we mentioned the home page that contains information about professional cooking schools throughout the United States. Well, here's that page's twin sister: cooking schools that are just plain fun (which is what it says in the page title). Here you can find a description of schools by state and offerings at such wonderful programs as The Great Chefs at Robert Mondavi Winery, California Culinary Academy (California), Chef Allen's (North Miami Beach, Florida), Le Panier (Houston, Texas), and Peter Kump's School of Culinary Arts (New York). Here's a note about Kump's school, which offers many different types of classes for varied times ranging from one day to one week to a full training program—there are courses for the beginner or the advanced nonprofessional, but also a complete program for the professional.

MARGARET COWAN DIRECT

http://www.portal.ca/~mcowan/

If you're lucky enough, you may be able to combine a vacation in Europe with cooking class via Margaret Cowan's 57 different school holidays, including vacations in Venice, Umbria, Tuscany, and Rome (see opposite page). A description of each comes as a book, but you can get a good feeling for what the experience is like by examining her home page and some of the links that she has included. The titles of the trips, such as Cook with a Tuscan Family on Their Farm in the Hills Near Pisa or Cooking in a Saracen Tower on a Seaside Cliff in Heavenly Amalfi (South), sound fascinating and a bit romantic to boot.

JANE BUTEL'S COOKING SCHOOL

(http://www.pecosvalley.com/school.html)

Our last school is a local one that has all the features nonprofessionals are looking for: an established track record, weekend and week-long classes, full participation, and small classes. Jane Butel starting offering classes in Sante Fe in 1983 and features traditional New Mexico cooking. As an added treat, each weekend class begins with a cocktail party followed by the cooking and each week-long class begins with a dinner at a well-known restaurant. The 5-day courses end each day at about 2 P.M., and the rest of the day and the evening are left for other activities.

LISTS OF SCHOOLS AND CLASSES

Here are some other links to lists of cooking schools.

The Professional and Avocational Cooking Schools (http://www.foodshow.com/e03.htm) home page contains a list of both professional and avocational cooking schools, with no links to any home pages, but addresses and phone numbers. Another list well worth exploring is ChefNet (http://www.chefnet.com/wine/fwo17.html).

Margaret Cowan Direct Ltd.

Margaret Cowan in Trimani Wine Bar, Rome

Welcome gourmet travellers! Now you can discover over 57 decadent cooking school holidays in Italy all in one book.

Prices range from bargains to luxury. How would you like to live and cook with an Italian family in their beautifully renovated, 13th century farmhouse on a Tuscan hilltop for about $1200 U.S. a week all inclusive? This once-in-a-lifetime experience is one of 15 "Great Deals" you'll find in the new, **"Your Guide to 57 Decadent Cooking Holidays in Italy"**.

I'm the author, Margaret Cowan, your expert on culinary travel in Italy. I welcome you and invite you to enjoy all the **FREE** gifts offered here. Saluti & buon appetito!

- "Your Guide to 57 Decadent Cooking Holidays in Italy"
- "Sensational Recipes from Italian Cooking School Chefs"
- Cooking School of the Month
- FREE Recipe of the Month
- Order Form
- Italian Gastronomic Trivia of the Month
- FREE Sample of One Cooking School Listing
- Who is Margaret Cowan?
- Frequently Asked Questions About Cooking Schools in Italy
- Join Mailing List

Quote of the Month:

"Tortellini are more essential than the sun for Saturday and the love of a woman."
Anonymous, Gazetta di Bologna, December 1874.

◄ JUST FOR KIDS ►

Recipes Just for Kids
•
Other Kids' Cooking Activities

The legendary American chef James Beard tells of working in the kitchen as a child, at his mother's side. It's not unusual for people who love to cook, be they amateur or professional, to have wonderful stories to tell about food and their childhood be it holiday celebrations, baking cookies, or trying a new food for the first time.

The lesson in having kids cook is that they learn how to enjoy preparing and sharing food with and for others. Cooking lessons can also be used to indirectly teach basic math skills, cooperation, responsibility, and reading. Some wonderful cookbooks for kids are available, but there are also some wonderful resources online.

RECIPES JUST FOR KIDS

Just for kids? Who's kidding whom? Maybe these are just for kids to make, but certainly not just for kids to eat! This is by far the largest category of entries you'll find on the Internet. Many of these are the perfect recipes for children who are just starting to cook because the ingredients are easy to find, the recipes are easy to follow, and the final results taste good enough to encourage children to continue cooking.

Start with the Cooking with Kids! home page (http://www.intex.net/~dlester/pam/recipe/recipeskids.html), shown on the next page, which contains links to other kids' cooking sites (we include them all in this discussion) as well as bunch of recipes such as Cinnamon Raisin Bread, Green Spaghetti, and (a favorite among children learning to count) Number salad (1 handful of toasted coconut, 2 tablespoons of orange juice concentrate, 3 orange sections, 4 apple slices . …you get the idea).

Black & Decker (the tool people) seem to be into everything, and they've touched on children in the kitchen as well. Their Cooking with Kids home page (http://www.blackanddecker.com/household/recipes/kidcook/strawberry.shtml) contains recipes such as Baked Stuffed Apples, Cheese Dogs with Sauerkraut, Conehead Cuties, Strawberry Heaven, and the adult taste in a kid-sized recipe, Jailhouse Rock Bars (butterscotch and chocolate chips, condensed milk, walnuts and marshmallows—an easy recipe but for older children because it includes some heating of ingredients).

🔥Cooking With Kids !🔥

We are always adding new things to this page, so bookmark it and visit often!

★Go to the Cooking With Kids Recipes!★

Kid's Recipe Links

★The Kitchen Link - Kids in the Kitchen

★Holiday: Halloween Recipes

★Halloween Tricks And Treats

★Halloween Recipes

★Recipes for Parents, children & babies

★Easy Recipes For Kids

★Baking With M&M's Recipes

★Kid's Cafe - Breakfast Recipes

★Kid's Cafe - Lunch Recipes

★Kid's Cafe - Dinner Recipes

★Kid's Cafe - Dessert Recipes

★Kid's cafe - Snacks Recipes

★Pear Bear Healthy Kid Recipes

SAFETY FOR KIDS (http://www.kraftfoods.com/html/rules.html)

What makes kids such wonderful and curious cooks also leaves them at risk for accidents in the kitchen. Very young children should of course be supervised at all times in the kitchen and even older children (5 years and older) should be familiar with the following rules, which they can easily understand.

1. Wash your hands with soap and water before you begin.
2. Read the whole recipe carefully before starting. If you don't understand any part, ask an adult to help you.
3. Collect all the ingredients and equipment you need for the recipe before you start to cook.
4. Do one step of the recipe at time. Do not skip steps.
5. Ask an adult to help you when a recipe calls for boiling water; a microwave, stove, or oven; or a sharp knife.
6. Measure carefully, using the correct equipment.
7. Use the size of pan called for in the recipe.
8. Follow the times given in the recipe. If a recipe says chill for one hour, be sure to chill the mixture for at least one hour.
9. Clean up when you are finished!
10. Most important, share your tasty creations with family and friends.

YAN CAN COOK (AND SO CAN KIDS) http://www.2way.com/food/egg/egg0296/kidscook.html

You may know about the popular "Yan Can Cook" show on PBS. Here's what he has to say about cooking with children and his annual show for children.

They [children] learn not to waste anything. When you buy a chicken, when you buy a bunch of celery, you don't have to throw anything away. Everything can be used. So when kids learn to cook, they also learn not to waste anything, they learn to appreciate things in life, in nature, rather than packaged foods. It's a learning process, an educational process.

OTHER KIDS' COOKING ACTIVITIES

A really interesting approach to children and cooking can be found at the Kids Cooking Club (http://www.kidscook.com/ recipe1.htm). This is a monthly club where a cooking project is delivered to your home—complete ingredients, recipes, craft projects, a cooking gift, and a newsletter—for $12.95 per month. An example of a month's goodies (for October 1996) includes recipes for a Halloween party including Black Widow Spider Cupcakes. Membership would make a nice holiday gift for any child.

Finally, there's "Hey Kids! What's Cooking?", a video cookbook from Merritt Creations (`http://www.backdoor.com/merritt/welcome.html`). The home page includes a monthly special recipe, all of which require a minimum of adult help. The month we checked (October) was French Cheese Bread, with an easy to follow and complete recipe. One of the nicest features of this tape is that it includes a demonstration of over 40 different cooking skills, concepts, and techniques that provide those basic skills that last a lifetime.

COOKING SOFTWARE

Commercial Software

•

Shareware

•

Macintosh Shareware

•

Windows and DOS Programs

This chapter is different from the others. Here, we're going to list software that's available online as well as that you might purchase commercially. Because it would be impossible to thoroughly review each of the offerings, we'll just accompany each mention with a brief description.

Two general categories of software are available. The first is for the amateur cook. Examples of software that belongs in this category are recipe CDs, software for children, and celebrity software (which actor cooks what). The second is for the professional. Examples of software that falls into this category are kitchen reference packages, accounting software, and food and beverage management tools. We'll look at software that falls into both of these categories.

COMMERCIAL SOFTWARE

Commercial cooking software for the amateur and professional has only been available for a few years, but it seems to be catching up quickly to even the most sophisticated and well-designed offerings in other areas such as applications and games.

For example, in the celebrity category, there's Cooking with Dom Deluise (from Allegro software at *www.allegronm.com*). His opening arms on the opening screen you see on the next page characterize the humor that's contained in the double set of CDs that contain hundreds of recipes for meats, fish, poultry, pasta, vegetables, salads, desserts, and breads, and include features such as

- shopping list generation,
- recipe printing,
- an electronic timer (now if you could only fit your PC next to the stove),
- a calculator, and
- a recipe card format.

The screen on the following page shows the recipe for Calzone, a delicious, baked combination of vegetables and cheese baked in a soft bread shell. You can see at the bottom of the screen the convenient buttons for printing the recipe, accessing an ingredients list, and more. This set of disks contains recipes, but also lots of fun from Dom's introduction (a video of him at the grocery store) down to the audio effects including "Bon Appetit" and burps!

Several companies seem to be taking a strong interest in the commercial cooking software area with a number of established and new products for both amateurs and professionals. Here's a brief description of some of the offerings for amateurs. You can find out more about each of these products at the Software on *Food & Wine* home page at http://www.bpe.com/food/software/foodwine/index.html.

The Great American Cooking CD (from Multicom Publishing) offers more than 500 recipes selected from community cookbooks and tested in the *Better Homes and Gardens* kitchens.

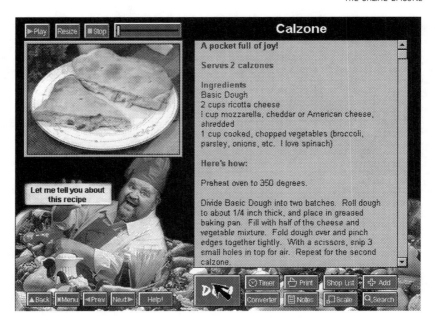

The Gardens Healthy Cooking CD (from Multicom Publishing) is based on *Better Homes and Gardens' New Dieter's Cookbook* and contains 400 recipes and uses full-motion video to illustrate cooking techniques.

The Digital Gourmet Classic (from Teletypsetting) contains over 1,000 recipes, can be added to and searched, and is accompanied by a nutritional analysis feature.

The *Family Circle Cookbook* (from Pinpoint Publishing) offers over 700 recipes with 230 sample menus, along with nutritional information for each of the recipes.

Recipe Manager (Hopkins Technology) takes an interesting approach in that it is compatible with the indices produced by *Food & Wine, Gourmet, Bon Appetit, Cooking Light,* and *Eating Well.* You can manage recipes and access these indices to find references to where recipes might be (but not the recipes themselves). Also, the indices are sold separately.

You can find information about ordering these and other software products at `http://www.bpe.com/food/software/foodwine/index.html`.

All of the software products discussed so far are for Windows or DOS. For you Macintosh users, MasterCookMac (from Arion

Software) contains over 1,000 recipes and has all those features you expect from a well-designed recipe program, such as setting up menus, generating shopping lists, searching by recipes for various criteria, and analyzing costs.

Lifestyle Cooking Software (http://www.lifeware.com/coming.htm) has recently entered the market with several high-quality products. One such new product, *The Southern Living Cookbook*, offers over 1,300 of "the South's most inviting recipes," plus preparation tips and the techniques necessary to prepare these dishes. There's even mood music and photographs to make this a total experience.

Another new offering form Lifestyle is *Cook It Light*, based on the ideas and recipes of Jeanne Jones, a syndicated columnist and writer on healthy cooking. This CD contains over 700 recipes with photos and videos.

Lifestyle's other offerings contain a complete set of Betty Crocker cookbooks including the *Microwave Cookbook, Shortcut Cooking for the SmartCook*, and the *Low-Fat, Low-Cholesterol Cookbook*. You can also find information on the Lifestyle home page about *The Healthy Heart Cookbook, Francis Bissell's Times of London Cookbook*, and *Mrs. Beeton's Book of Cookery and Household Management*.

Billed as "The Most Delicious CD-ROM You'll Ever Own," Digital Gourmet (http://www.teletype.com/gourmet/nutrition.html), brings thousands of recipes to Macintosh and Window platforms as well as hand-held computers such as the Apple Newton Personal Digital Assistant (or PDA). The CD includes hundreds of recipes plus extensive nutritional information even down to plant protein and percentage of calories from fat.

For the professional, there's Culinary Software Services (http://www.foodstuff.com/pearl/cul-sof.html), offering software for food services operations, but also software for the student. For example, for $295 you can own the Escoffier software program, which contains four modules that help manage any food endeavor including Recipe & Menu Costing, Inventory Control, Nutritional Analysis, and Employee Records & Scheduling modules. There's also a less ambitious entry-level package for around $1200.

Culinary Software also offers software (Escoffier Student) for teaching students in culinary programs. The program teaches basic computer concepts and contains tools for recipe creation and management, costing out ingredients, menu development, and inventory control. There are recipe databases available that are designed to be used with the Escoffier software.

On a more consumer note, this same company offers Culinary Tip of the Day (for Windows), where a tip appears on the computer screen every day.

CALCMENU for DOS from EGS Software at `http://ourworld.compuserve.com/homepages/egs_calcmenu/` offers Stock & Inventory Control, Barcode Management, Menu Planning, Supplies & Purchase Order, and Recipe Database modules.

Finally, there's Cooking with Kids (for Windows) from Allegro (`http://www.alegronm.com`). When the cursor becomes the shape of a wooden spoon and you can list recipe categories such as Anytime Desserts and Sweets or Super-Super Snacks and Drinks, you know you're in the right place—especially if you're over 6. This is a nicely designed, sound- and video-enhanced introduction to cooking for children. Because almost every child likes to cook, for a myriad of reasons, this is a good introduction to important issues such as safety around the kitchen, a glossary, and even what you'll need and how to use utensils. Special features include 25 full-motion videos of kids actually cooking, the Cook-a-matic, where kids can mix up their own concoctions without messing up the kitchen, and tips on safety, kitchen computing, and using appliances.

SHAREWARE

Here's the second major class of offerings. The concept behind shareware is to try before you buy, which means in some cases you get a free trial period and then the software becomes unusable (because of programming by the author). In other cases, it means that you can use it for as long as you like and you are encouraged to pass it on to friends and others who might be interested. Some shareware authors ask for a small registration fee to be paid if you plan on keeping and using the software. This supports the author and allows further software development.

You can find shareware on any of the three big services we talk about in *The Online Epicure* or on the Internet. Use the **Go** or **Find** commands and the keyword *shareware*, and you'll find tools such as CompuServe's File Finder. Once the keyword *cooking* is entered, you'll get back recipes, artwork, and lists of all the equipment someone else thinks you need in your kitchen! You'll then have to download the files in order to use them.

The shareware concept really works. Some of the most used utilities in the personal computer world (such as PKZIP, which allows you to compress and uncompress large files) are shareware.

We'll cover shareware programs designed for Windows (which can also run DOS software) and Macintosh. To get these programs and download them, you'll have to use your Internet browser and ftp to the location that accompanies the software description, then download the file. Most of the software consists of collections of recipes, but there are several cooking applications as well.

There are several different ways to find the shareware that is mentioned here. In order for you to use this shareware, these files have to be downloaded from the computer on which they are stored to your computer. Go to the home page or ftp site that is mentioned in the description and then search through the page to find a mention of the file you want to download. When you click on the file that you want, you will be shown a dialog box and asked where you want to store the file as you see below.

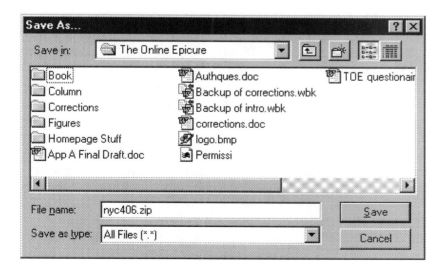

Once the file is downloaded, it may have to be expanded (if it was transferred in a compressed format). That usually consists of double-clicking on the file name (which usually ends with an .exe for Windows and DOS programs). The file expands by itself. In the case of Macintosh, the program should self-install once double-clicked.

Another method is to go to www.shareware.com and search by keywords such as *cooking, recipes*, and *food*. See what you find. Once a file is identified, click on the one you want and download it to your computer.

Finally, some shareware requires other applications for it to be used. For example, many Macintosh programs require you to have HyperCard installed on your computer. Some Windows programs require a specific database such as Paradox or Access. Just be sure to read the shareware description when you go to the site at which it is located.

MACINTOSH SHAREWARE

Here are 10 great software products that you might want to try. There are literally hundreds of others from which you can select after completing a search using an search engine.

MacChef Stack is a HyperCard stack designed to archive recipe text files that have come from listserv and Usenet groups such as rec.food. recipes. FTP to mirror.apple.com and download the file named mac-chef-stack.hqx.

Recipe Finder Deluxe contains 40 recipes from the author's kitchen and issued with the database, FoxPro. FTP to mirror.apple.com and download the file named recipe-dfinder-dlx-301.hqx.

Amy's Recipes 2.4 is a color recipe program that has lots of features and includes hundreds of recipes that you can organize anyway you want. FTP to mirror.apple.com and download the file named amys-recipes-24.hqx.

Brewer's Notebook is a program to help homebrewers organize their recipes and do brewing-related calculations. The program allows for the recording of important information such as ingredients, specific gravity, temperature, and more. FTP to `mirror.apple.com` and download the file named `brewers-notebook-11.hqx`.

A very easy-to-use cookbook (that has no name!), which requires FileMaker Pro to use, allows you to enter your own recipes in a free format and select from over 280 other recipes. Great graphics and excellent search tools characterize this shareware. FTP to `mirror.apple.com` and download the file named `cook-ware-ii-fm.hqx`.

The Recipe Box is a meal management system that includes a recipe database, meal planner, grocery list planner, calorie chart, and more. FTP to `mirror.apple.com` and download the file named `recipe-box.hqx`.

If you want to print your recipes or others on to 3 x 5-inch index cards for perfect storage, try Computer Cuisine 3.2. It works with FileMaker Pro and includes 125 recipes, an expanded print menu, color printing, large and small printing options, a recipe notes area, conversion tools, and more. FTP to `ftp.amug.org` and download the file named `cook-ware-ii-fm.hqx`.

If you want to know if what you eat is healthy, try one of the more than 200 screens provided by VegieCard. Recipes, great illustrations, and nutritional information are included in this HyperCard Stack. FTP to `ftp.amug.org` and download the file named `vegiecard-1.25.sit.hqx`.

If your goal is to find out how much fat is in the food you eat or serve, then you should download Fat Tracker. It lets you define and track daily calories, fat in grams, cholesterol, and sodium. You can add your own items to the already existing database of 800. FTP to `ftp.amug.org` and download the file named `fat-tracker.sit.hqx`.

Bartender's Dream offers a HyperCard stack with 137 recipes and allows you to add your own. FTP to `ftp.amug.org` and download the file named `bartenders-dream.sit.hqx`.

Laughing Bird Restaurant offers recipes collected from 23 different restaurants in the Los Angeles and San Diego area. FTP to `ftp.amug.org` and download the file named `vegiecard-1.25.sit.hqx`. FTP to `ftp.amug.org` and download the file named `laughingbird-restaurant4.04.sit.hqx`.

WINDOWS AND DOS PROGRAMS

Here are more shareware products designed specifically for Windows and DOS. These may take some time to download (especially if you have a slow modem), but they're worth looking at as an alternative to strictly commercial products.

Now You're Cooking (formerly The Grocery Consumer from Food for Thought software) is the shareware product, and as comments on the Internet seem to indicate, it's the shareware leader. First, you can download it from The Now You're Cooking home page at `http://www.intergate.net:80/chtml/ghauser/gcinfo.html`. It comes with 2,000 importable Meal Master™ files (the next program reviewed) from all over the world.

This is the third version of the program and offers literally hundreds of features, including these:

A toolbar for quick use
Context-sensitive help
Autocategorizing of recipes
Extensive meal planning
Unit conversion

Shopping list aisle sorting
Coupon management
Shopping list comparisons
  across stores
Extensive printing options

You can see the Recipe Editor screen, where a recipe can be selected, directions revealed and printed, quantities changed, and ingredients listed in a variety of different ways. All these recipes can be edited as well. This is a fabulous program that costs $25 for registration (there's a 60-day free evaluation) and belongs in any amateur or professional online epicure's toolbox.

Another exciting program is Meal-Master from EpiSoft, Inc., and authored by Scott Welliver, which manages over 58,000 recipes in Meal-Master format, all of which you can download at the same home page. This DOS database (available on the Meal-Master home page at `http://ourworld.compuserve.com/homepages/s_welliver`) is shareware and is in version 8, and although the interface is not as exciting as Windows, a DOS-based program definitely has advantages such as speed and memory demands. You can run a DOS-based program in any version of Windows. (Incidentally, a later version number usually means that the bugs have been worked out and there's been lots of time to add features.)

You can select and download recipes from Meal-Master in a variety of ways. One is to click by ingredient. The file containing that number or recipes (such as the 356 using slivered almonds) will then be downloaded to whatever location you specify on your computer. You then open the Meal-Master program and use whatever recipe you want.

Besides the recipes that are available on the Meal-Master home page, there are other depositories of recipes, including those links located on the Now You're Cooking home page. Here are the file names, each containing about 1,000 recipes. The first column is general, and the second lists files of recipes for specific foods such as Greek and soup. You can spend all day having fun with these and it's a great tool to use when planning a dinner party or a buffet, or even a quiet dinner for two.

- `mm13000a.zip`
- `mm13000b.zip`
- `mm13000c.zip`
- `mm13000d.zip`
- `mm13000e.zip`
- `mm13000f.zip`
- `mm13000g.zip`
- `mm13000h.zip`
- `mm13000i.zip`
- `mm13000j.zip`
- `mm13000k.zip`

- `Diabetic.zip` 930 (diabetic recipes)
- `Holiday.zip` (for the holiday season)
- `Kids.zip` 205 (recipes for kids)
- `Mexican.zip` (yep, you guessed it!)
- `Mmbread.zip`
- `Mm_greek.zip`
- `Mm_vegan.zip` (vegetarian)
- `Mmdrinks.zip`
- `Mmsoup.zip`
- `Choclate.zip` (for chocolate lovers)
- `Cookbook.zip` (1986 Usenet Cookbook)

From My Kitchen is another excellent example of creative shareware. You download a fully functional copy that is good for 90 days, which should be plenty of time for you to find out if it's a program you want to keep. As you can see here, you can use this software to enter and import recipes and use the utility and the enormous recipe list as you create your own. It's not only a complete recipe management tool, but it's great fun to use. We got From My Kitchen from CIS. The file name is `FMKIT100.zip`.

Some other Windows and DOS-based shareware programs you should consider follow.

- Cookbook stores, prints, and organized recipes. FTP to ftp.coast.net and download the file named `cookbk22.zip`.
- Barman offers a recipe editor (with recipes), plus lots of valuable information. FTP to `ftp.winsite.com` and download the file named `barman2.zip`.

- Recipe Manager allows you to input and manage an unlimited number of recipes. FTP to `ftp.winsite.com` and download the file named `rbw250sc.zip`.
- A search engine that contains over 750 drink recipes can be found at `winsite.com`. The file name is `mmm.exe`.

WHAT MAKES A GOOD RECIPE PROGRAM?

As you can see by our summary in this chapter, recipe software comes in every shape and size, and for every type of operating system (such as Mac or DOS), but how do you select one? Here are some tips.

- Be sure that the software matches your computer's operating system.
- Be sure that your computer meets the system requirements, especially as far as memory and disk storage space are concerned.
- Look for special features you may want such as nutritional analysis, whether other recipes can be imported, conversion tools, and availability of upgrades.
- See if technical support will be available if you need help in installation or use.
- Try to find out if the recipes that are listed have actually been tested. Nothing is more disappointing than following the instructions word for word and ending up with a mess.
- Most of us don't have a computer in our kitchen, so look for features that will make the program "kitchen friendly," such as being able to print out recipes.
- Finally, keep searching the newsgroups and surfing the Internet to find new products that might better fit your needs.

APPENDIX

E nter any one of the following URLs in your browser and press return to go to that homepage. These links are available through *The Online Epicure* homepage at www.onlinepicure.com.

20 reasons chocolate is better than sex	http://www.writepage.com/chocolat.htm?
21st Century Mall	http://www.21stcenturyplaza.com/
36 upstate New York wineries	http://fallcrk.tc.cornell.edu/Entertainment/Winefest/wineries.html
4,000 Internet providers	http://thelist.iworld.com/
50 Great Homebrewing Tips	http://mgfx.com/homebrew/hb50tips/index.htm
800-Microbrew	http://www.800-microbrew.com/
Adventures in Dining	http://www.go-dining.com/recipes.html
Adventures in Food	http://www.shopnet.prodigy.com/
Agricultural and Production Information	http://www.weather.net/roemerwx/publications/tradewinds/tw-jan-95/coffee.html
Alaska Seafood Cookbook	http://www.state.ak.us/local/akpages/COMMERCE/asmihp.htm
Alaska Seafood Direct	http://www.alaska.net/~asd/
Alcoholic drinks	http://www2/Southwind.net/~willie/DrinksListing/index/Ingred/GrainAlcohol.html
All about caffeine and tea	http://eMall.com/Republic/Tea.html
All-in-One Search	http://www.albany.net/allinone/
Allegro	http://www.alegronm.com
AltaVista	http://www.altavista.digital.com/
Amazon Books	http://www.amazon.com
American Cake Decorating	http://www.cakemag.com
American Heart Association	http://www.amhrt.org/pubs/ahadiet.html
American Homebrewers Association	http://www.aob.org/aob/aob.html#AHA
American Wine	http://www.foodwine.com/food/wine/
Angostura bitters	http://www.caribinfo.com/angostura/angosdes.html
Anna's	http://www.culinaria.com/freeaccess/catalog1/a/annasBarbecueSauce.html
Appetizer Recipes	http://godzilla.eecs.berkeley.edu/recipes/appetizers/
Appetizer Recipes	http://foodnet.fic.ca/recipes/appet1.html
Arthur's Restaurant	http://bonviv.com/home/arthurs/winelst.htm
Artichoke Cheese Strata	http://www.mal.com/~squealer/links/recipe.html
Ask the Dietitian	http://www.hoptechno.com/rdindex.htm
Ask the Dietitian (hint)	http://www.hoptechno.com/cookhint.htm
Association of Brewers	http://www.aob.org/aob/aob.html
Ateliers Reunnis Caddie	http://www.hospitalitynet.nl/vlist/caddie.htm
AT&T toll-free directory	http://www.tollfree.att.net/cgi-bin/plsqf_opcode.pl
Atrocities homepage	http://www.aus.xanadu.com/GlassWings/food/recipe.html
Baby's Place Coffee Bar	http://www.vacation3.com/babys.html
Bajas Tour ?96	http://home.sn.no/~gwalther/bajas.htm
Bartlett's Quotations	http://www.columbia.edu/acis/bartleby/bartlett/
Basement beer crowd at	http://www.beerinfo.com/~jlock/beerads5.html
Beer & Brewing Index	http://www.beerinfo.com/~jlock/wwwbeer.html
Beer at Home	http://www.beerathome.com/~beer/
Beer Info Source	http://www.beerinfo.com/~jlock/beerinf3.html
Beer Institute	http://www.beerinst.org/
Beer Institute of course at	http://www.beerinst.org/inst/fun/cook.htm
Ben & Jerry's	http://www.benjerry.com/indexg.html
Best restaurants to east in Hanoi	http://vietconnection.com/Cooking/CNews2/chaca.htm
Beyond the French Riviera	http://www.beyond.fr/food/dishes.html

Bill Cupp's homepage	http://www.rmc.ca/~cupp/thought1.htm#chocolate
Black & Decker (Italian bread)	http://www.blackanddecker.com/household/recipes/bread/italian.shtm
Black & Decker	http://www.blackanddecker.com/household/recipes/bread/french.shtml
Bloomington Brewing Company, a microbrewery	http://bbc.bloomington.com
BPE	http://www.bpe.com/index.html
Brad at	http://www.math.okstate.edu/~kbradle/snacks/
Bread Basket Company at	http://www.pnh.mv.net/ipusers/basketman/baskets/bb-2.htm
Brewers Publications	http://www.aob.org/aob/bp/bp.html
Brewing Studies	http://www.aob.org/aob/contents.html#IBS
Brewin'	http://www.coffey.com/~brewshop/BBHome.html
breWorld at	http://www.breworld.com/
Bring Me My Dinner	http://www.townline.com/bmmd/bmmdcity.htm
Buckhead Coffee Houses/Coffee bar	http://www.buckhead.org/entertai/coffee.html
Butterball	http://www.butterball.com/
BYOB (Be Your Own Brewmaster)	http://www.byob.com/
Café a GoGo	http://www.illuminatus.com/fun/agogo/coffee_a_gogo.html
Campbell's Soups	http://www.campbellsoups.com/!!r05wa2M7dr05wa2M7d/books/Welcome2.html
Caviar	http://cybermal.com/caviar/cavrecip.htm
Centrale Lyon	http://www.ec-lyon.fr/Home.en/Rhone-Alpes/Lyon/Art_de_vivre/Cuisine/main.htm
Centre Point	http://www.csquare.com/1110/food/cook.html
Channel Index	http://fiddle.ee.vt.edu/proto/Entertainment/Food_and_Eating/Recipes/Seafood/
Chardonnay Golf Club	http://www.napavalley.com/napavalley/outdoor/chargolf/chargolf.html
Cheese and Wine Matching Page	http://www.sumaridge.com/wineconn/cheese.htm
Cheese Blintzes	http://ecep1.usl.edu/cajun/ent/10208.htm
Cheese Class	http://www.cheesemaking.com/recipes/
Cheese Information	http://www.wgx.com/cheesenet/info/
Cheese Links	http://www.wgx.com/cheesenet/links/
Cheese Literature homepage	http://www.wgx.com/cheesenet/lit/
Cheese!	http://www.crayola.cse.psu.edu:80/~jrichard/cheese/cheese.html
Cheese Recipes	http://www.cs.cmu.edu/~mjw/recipes/cheese/index.html
Cheesemaking 101 link	http://www.cheesemaking.com/intro/cheez101.htm
Cheesemaking Supply Company	http://www.cheesemaking.com/
CheeseNet	http://www.wgx.com/cheesenet/
Chef Celebration Tour	http://www.indianharvest.com/html/cheftour.html
ChefNet	http://www.chefnet.com/wine/fwol.html
Chicago Tribune	http://www.chicago.tribune.com/print/goodeat/current/goodeat.html
Chinese recipes	http://www.cs.cmu.edu/~mjw/recipes/ethnic/chinese/chinese.html
Chocolate listserve	http://www.qrc.com/~sholubek/choco/majrdomo.html
Chocolate	http://www.yahoo.com/Business_and_Economy/Companies/Food/Snacks/Candy/Chocol
Chocolate companies	http://www.candyusa.org/store.html
Chocolate Reviews	http://www.hhhh.org/cloister/chocolate/reviews/
Chocolate Talk	http://www.kaiwan.com/~perew/choctalk.html
Christmas Recipes	http://holiday.ritech.com/christmas/recipe.html
Christmas Stars at	http://www.gil.com.au/ozkidz/Christmas/star.html
Christopher's Recipes	http://www.christophers.com/hotncold.html
Chocolate Talk	http://www.kaiwan.com/~perew/choctalk.html
Cloister's Chocolate Review Page	http://www.hhhh.org/cloister/chocolate/
Coffee	http://ice.bae.uga.edu/dept/ugrads/lerch/coffee.html
Coffee A Go Go	http://www.illuminatus.com/fun/agogo/ coffee_a_gogo.html
Coffee A Go Go (A contest)	http://www.illuminatus.com/fun/agogo/free.html
Coffee by Country	http://www.lucidcafe.com/lucidcafe/bycountry.html
Coffee Link	http://www-personal.engin.umich.edu/~cbrokaw/
Coffee Lover's Heaven	http://www.edu.yorku.ca/~tcs/~adawson/coffee.html

Coffee Quest	http://www.inetcafe.com/bev/cq/coffhome.htm
Coffee Shops and Desserts	http://www.abilene.com/dining/tablecloth/bakery.html
Coffee Comisso's Market cookbooks	http://www.eden.com/~bgg/cookbks.html
Columbus' Quincentennial macaroni and cheese	http://www.ilovepasta.org/recipes/meatless/505.html
Comisso's Market	http://www.commisso.com/recipe/salad.html
Cooking	http://www.byu.edu/acd1/ed/InSci/Projects/uvpcug/cooking.htm
Cooking Club	http://www.kidscook.com/recipe1.htm
Cooking for the Holidays	http://www.bpe.com/food/recipes/corn/holiday.html
Cooking Ragu	http://www.ragu.com
Cooking Schools/Institutes	http://www.kitchenlink.com/ref.html#CookingSchools/Institutes
Cooking with Beer homepage	http://www.dra.nl/~rubbeer/cookbook/index.html
Cooking with Beer	http://www.beerinst.org/inst/fun/cook.htm
Cooking with Kids	http://www.blackanddecker.com/household/recipes/kidcook/strawberry.s.html
Cooks' Corner	http://wchat.on.ca/merlene/cook.htm#recipe
Crab Salad	http://www.pwseafood.com/recipes/crsalad.htm
Crazy Homebrewers Club	http://www.netins.net/showcase/spsbeer/crazy/
Creations	http://www.backdoor.com/merritt/welcome.html
Creelers Recipe of the Week	http://www.demon.co.uk/creelers/recipe.html
CuisineNet	http://www.cuisinenet.com/
Cyber Recipes	http://www.cyberpages.com/RECIPE.htm
Cyber-Dine	http://www.cyber-view.com/cyber/state.html
Cybercafe	http://www.bid.com/bid/coffeeworld/java.html
CyberCalendar of Wine Events	http://www.wines.com/events1.html
CyberDiet	http://www.cyberdiet.com/
Dawn's homepage	http://www.hcc.cc.fl.us/services/staff/dawn/choco.htm
Dave (McKeown)	http://www.cs.cmu.edu/afs/cs/usr/maps/www/traditions/bbq.html
David Henderson's Page of French Recipes	http://jeffco.k12.co.us/dist_ed/spring96/onlinec/dahender/recipes.html
DeJeans's Beer Page	http://imol.vub.ac.be/~jqdoumen/ElJuanElIncredibile.html
Delicious Chocolate Recipes	http://www.go-dining.com/recipes.html
Digital Gourmet	http://www.teletype.com/gourmet/nutrition.html
dineAmerica	http://www.dineamerica.com/
Dining Out Guide	http://www.record-journal.com/rest/restndx.html
Dinner's Coop	http://dinnercoop.cs.cmu.edu/cgi-bin/aglimpse/01/Recipes?query= sauce&whole=on&errors=0&maxfiles=100&maxlines=Internet E-mail
Dr. Cheese	http://www.wgx.com/cheesenet/info/drcheese.html
Ecola's 24-Hour Newsstand	http://www.ecola.com/news/
Egg Rolls	http://www.vietconnection.com/Arts/cooking/recipes/Appetizer/eggrolls.htm
EGS Software	http://ourworld.compuserve.com/homepages/egs_calcmenu/
Emeal Restaurant Listings	http://www.emeal.com/
Epicurean Thyme	http://members.tripod.com/~Epicurean/index.html
Epicurious Drinking	http://www.epicurious.com/d_drinking/d00_home/drinking.html
Epicurious Food	http://www.epicurious.com/a_home/a00_home/home.html
Equipment	http://www.taylor-company.com/cook/cook.htm
ESP Mail Program	http://www.esp.co.uk/
Ethel M. Chocolates Company	http://www.ethelm.com/
Ethnic Foods	http://www.cyber-kitchen.com/pgethnic.htm
Ethiopian Jewish Food and Recipes	http://www.cais.com/nacoej/13.html
Fargo's Iced Mocha	http://www.qrc.com/~sholubek/choco/dcchoco.htm#fargo
Festival and Events homepage	http://www.w2.com/docs2/act/festivals/festivals.html
Fit and Healthy Lifestyles	http://odin.cc.pdx.edu/~psu03561/pm.htm
FITE	http://www.bright.net/~fite/

Japanese Tea Garden	http://www.belmont.gov/orgs/alumni/smoke_f95_centen_tea.html
Jenny's Shrimp Salad	http://www-ssc.igpp.ucla.edu/~newbury/recipes/shrimpsalad.html
Jewish Cooking by Robert Sternberg	http://www.aronson.com/Judaica/yidcook.html
Jewish Cooking in America	http://www.randomhouse.com/special/passover/tastes.html
Jewish Food Recipes Archives	http://www.eskimo.com/~jefffree/recipes/
Jewish Recipes	http://soar.berkeley.edu/recipes/ethnic/jewish/
Jim's Blues N' Brews	http://www.cloud9.net/~leftwich/
Julie's Low & Fat Free Resource List	http://www.eskimo.com/~baubo/lowfat.html
Jumping Pad	http://academy.bastad.se/~recipes/JumpingPad.html
Just Plain Fun	http://www.bpe.com/food/reference/cookingschools/cont.html
Kansas City Barbecue Society	http://www.barbeque.com/champs/
Karin's Cooking Stuff	http://www.karinrex.com/cooking.html
Kentucky Herald-Leader	http://www.kentuckyconnect.com/heraldleader/restaurants/index.htm
Kids Cooking Club	http://www.kidscook.com/recipe1.htm
Kids Recipes at	http://www.god.co.uk/ynet/text/choc.html
Kids! homepage	http://www.intex.net/~dlester/pam/recipe/recipeskids.html
Kosher Express	http://www.marketnet.com/kosher/recipes.html
Kugel	http://www.jcn18.com/food/bt6.htm
Kugel and coffee cake	http://www.jewish.com/bk951110/cook.htm
Lady's Club	http://godzilla.eecs.berkeley.edu/recipes/bean-salads/
Larocca's in Tucson, AZ	http://www.ibs-net.com/tucson/rest/larocca4.htm
Le Cordon Bleu	http://sunsite.unc.edu/expo/restaurant/history.html
Lifestyle Cooking Software	http://www.lifeware.com/coming.htm
Library of Congress homepage	http://lcweb.loc.gov/
Lipton Tea folks	http://www.lipton.com/june-bev.html
Little Dave's Recipe of the Week	http://www.lainet.com/~eatfish/recipe.htm
Look for the recipe at	http://www.harpercollins.com/kids/kwan.htm#c.
Low-Fat, High-flavor Dining	http://www.bpe.com/food/recipes/pappas/
Low-Fat Living	http://www.xe.net/lowfat/editor.htm
Low-Fat Living homepage	http://www.xe.net/lowfat/
Low-Fat Living homepage tip	http://www.xe.net/lowfat/tips/tip_0001.htm
Low-Fat Vegetarian Archive	http://www.fatfree.com/
Lucid Café	http://www.lucidcafe.com/lucidcafe/
Macaroni and Cheese	http://www.lib.uchicago.edu/keith/cookbook/recipes/macaroni-and-cheese.html
Macaroni and Cheese	http://www.kuow.washington.edu/wkdy/recipes/r27.htm
Mad Italian Chemist Scientist	http://www.mtech.edu/wwwclass/fboroni/recipes.htm
Mall Direct	http://www.mdbl.com/shoplinks.htm
Malls, Shopping and Food sites	http://www.swcbc.com/SHOP.html
Mama Cucin's homepage	http://www.ragu.com
Maple Leaf Prime Chicken	http://www.goprime.com/recipe/asian/
Margaret Cowan Direct at	http://www.portal.ca/~mcowan/
Mars Kraft	http://www.mars.com.
Martha	http://www.esva.net/martha/salads.htm
Martha's Dessert Recipes at	http://www.esva.net/martha/dessert.htm
Michael Aichlmary	http://www.culinaria.com/collectedRecipes/sauces.html
Mimi's Cyber Kitchen	http://www.cyber-kitchen.com/
Mr. Cheese's World of Cheese!	http://www.princeton.edu/~gprudhom/cheese/
My Italian Heritage	http://iaswww.com/fndraise.html
Mystiqu Krew of Brew Club	http://www.neosoft.com/~dosequis/homepage.html
Nacho Style Macaroni and Cheese	http://www.eat.com/cookbook/light/lt-nacho-macaroni-cheese.html
Napa Valley Virtual Visit	http://www.napavalley.com/cgi-bin/home.o
Napa Valley Wineries	http://www.freerun.com/napavalley/mwinerie.html

National Confectioners Association and the Chocolate Manufaturers Association	http://www.candyusa.org/stats.html
Native Foods	http://indy4.fdl.cc.mn.us/~isk/food/recipes.html
Natural Resource Directory	http://www.itlnet.com/natural/nrd/sect3c.html
Nestle	http://www.nestle.com/
New England Culinary Institute	http://www.neculinary.com/neci/welcome.htm
No title	http://www.shellcan.com/cmarket/appetiz.htm
Online Cookbook	http://www.hersheys.com/recipes/chocolate.pasta.recipes.html
Overeaters Anonymous	http://www.hiwaay.net/recovery/
Pam Williams	http://studio.bpe.com/food/recipes/hotchoc/two.html
ParentsPlace.com	http://www.parentsplace.com/readroom/recipes/recipes.html
Passover	http://www.bpe.com/food/recipes/fiszer/passover.html
Paula Giese	http://indy4.fdl.cc.mn.us/~isk/food/r_choc.html
Pennsylvania Culinary	http://www.pacul.com/
Phillip Goldwasser	http://www.jcn18.com/food/
Picture-Perfect Butterball Turkey	http://www.butterball.com/butterball/turkey.html
Pizza Hut restaurants	http://www.bigbook.com/showpage.cgi/3cc96c6c-0-0-0?page=listings_page&salesarea= NONE&company=pizza+hut&first=41
Professional Bartending School	http://www.netpage1.com/pbs/course.html
Professional Cooking Schools	http://www.bpe.com/food/reference/cookingschools/pro.html
Quick Breads moniker	http://ichef.cycor.ca/rec-food-recipes/breads/quick/quick.html
Quick Recipes	http://vd1.magibox.net/recipes/html/quick_recipes.html
Ragu	http://www.ragu.com/
Rec.Food.Recipes Archive	http://www.ichef.com/rec-food-recipes/recipe-archive.html
Recipes/Dining	http://www.dibbs.net./points/recipes.html
Restaurants	http://www.yahoo.com/Business_and_Economy/Companies/Restaurants/Directories/
Restaurant Central	http://www.cuisinenet.com/restaurant/index.html
Restaurant Reviews	http://www.yahoo.com/Entertainment/Food_and_Eating/Restaurants/Regional_Reviews/
Restaurant Reviews search tool	http://www.delcom.com/IRR/Feedback.html
Restaurants in Bloomington, Indiana	http://www.cs.indiana.edu/csgsa/outreach/restrev/dir.html
Rhode Island Restaurants	http://www.projo.com/horizons/postcards/review.html
Richards Restaurant Ranking	http://www.lagerling.se/rest.html
Robert's	http://www.infinet.com/~rbatina/other/candy.html
Safety for Kids	http://www.kraftfoods.com/html/rules.html
Sainsbury's	http://www.j-sainsbury.co.uk/recipes/seafood.html
Sally's Place	http://www.bpe.com/index.html
Seafood Recipe Archives	http://www.cs.cmu.edu/~mjw/recipes/seafood/seafood.html
Search Program	http://www.esp.co.uk/
Searchable Online Archive of Recipes	http://godzilla.eecs.berkeley.edu/recipes/
Secrets of great French chefs	http://users.aol.com/noisykids/private/secrets3.htm
Serving Wine	http://www.speakeasy.org/~winepage/wine.html
Seven Layer Bars	http://holiday.ritech.com/christmas/recipes/layerbar.html
Software on Food & Wine	http://www.bpe.com/food/software/foodwine/index.html
Soup Recipes	http://www.cc.gatech.edu/people/home/richb/Pumpkin/soups.html
Special Ingredients for Holiday Cooking	http://www.byerlys.com/bbag/Nov1995/featured.html
StarChefs	http://www.starchefs.com/chefscorner.html
StarChefs (professional schools)	http://www.starchefs.com/helpwanted.html
Start with Desserts & Jam Recipes	http://www.commisso.com/recipe/dessert.html
Stein Collectors International, Inc.	http://paterson.k12.nj.us/~steins/
Stylish Cooking	http://www.ny-works.com/rose/hat2.htm

Stylish Cooking Porcini Ristorante in Chicago	http://dine.package.com/chicago/porcini/wine.html
Sue's recipe server at	http://www.hubcom.com/cgi-win/recipe.exe/1
Sweet Seductions	http://connexion.parallax.co.uk/seduct
Sweet Sips	http://www.mkt-place.com/sweetsips/cthomas.html
Switzerland pizza	http://www.pizzanet.ch/
Sybil Carter's	http://ichef.cycor.ca/bbq/recipes/sauce/7219.html
T.C. Peabody's Espresso and Coffee Bar	http://home.revealed.net/peabody/bulk.html
Talley Vineyards	http://talley.websine.com
Tara's page	http://starburst.cbl.cees.edu/~tara/pastasalad.html
Taylor Cooking Equipment	http://www.taylor-company.com/cook/cook.htm
Tea As In Terrific	http://www.pt.hk-r.se/~di92jn/tea.html
Tea at	http://www.xroads.com/~pct/tea.html
Tea for Health and Enjoyment	http://www.teaworld.com/tea/
Tea in the Literature	http://kiwi.futuris.net/tea/teaquote.htm
Tea pages	http://bohr.physics.upenn.edu/~bush/tea_sites.html
Tea Vendor List	http://www.zumacafe.com/douglas/tea_vendor.html
The Bad Beer of the Month	http://207.43.106.35:80/badbeer/
The Beer Cap Collection	http://www.primenet.com/~jrblutt/beercap.html
The Beer Classifieds - Brewing Supplies	http://www.beerinfo.com/~jlock/beerads1.html
The Blue Directory	http://www.pvo.com/pvo/Food-Bev/
The Brewery	http://alpha.rollanet.org/
The Cheese Page	http://www.zennet.com/cheese/
The Chocolate Club	http://www.idma.com/chocolate/
The Chocolate Lover's Page	http://bc.emanon.net/chocolate/
The Christmas	http://www.harpercollins.com/kids/chri.htm
The Coffee Corner	http://www.tue.nl/wtb/wpa/se/klerk/cofcorn.htm
The Coffee Warehouse	http://www-015.connix.com/coffee/index.html
The Culinary Institute of America	http://www.thomson.com/partners/cia/default.html
The Dinner Coop	http://dinnercoop.cs.cmu.edu/dinnercoop/
The Duke Diet and Fitness Center	http://dmi-www.mc.duke.edu/dfc/home.html
The Electronic Newsstand	http://www.enews.com/
The Fat Boy Funhouse	http://www.geocities.com/SunsetStrip/3327/
The French Bread Basket Company	http://www.pnh.mv.net/ipusers/basketman/baskets/bb-2.htm
The French Culinary Institute	http://www.gourmetweb.com/search.html
The Great American Beer Club	http://www.greatclubs.com/beerclub.html
The Grocery Consumer homepage	http://www.intergate.net:80/chtml/ghauser/gcinfo.html
The High Holidays	http://www.jewish.com/bk950908/cook.htm
The Indian River Fruit Company	http://www.giftfruit.com/
The Internet Epicurean	http://www.epicurean.com
The New Wine Press	http://www.wines.com/winepress/press.html
The New York City Beer Guide	http://www.nycbeer.org/index.html
The Northern California Center for the Culinary Arts	http://www.omix.com/nccca/
The Northwest Portland Newspaper	http://elaine-1.teleport.com/~neighbor/restrv01.html
The Online Epicure	http://www.onlineepicure.com
The Palo Alto Weekly	http://www.service.com/PAW/thisweek/restaurants/1996_Sep_18.mini_reviews.html
The Pasta homepage	http://www.food.italynet.com/pasta/default1.htm
The Professional and Vocational Cooking Schools	http://www.foodshow.com/e03.htm
The Professional Chef's Culinary Assistant	http://www.whytel.com/ftp/users/chefnet/

The Pumpkin Patch Cookbook	http://www.cc.gatech.edu/people/home/richb/cookbook.html
The Recipes Folder!	http://english-www.hss.cmu.edu/recipes/
The Shaw Guide	http://www.shawguides.com/shacookinq.html
The Tea Business	http://www.asiainfo.com/plaza/hallway/Tuhsu-tea/eng/tea.html
The Tea Page	http://www.nitehawk.com/bnielsen/
The Times of Calumet	http://www.calunet.com/calunet/restaurants/restaurants.html
The Vegetarian Society UL	http://www.veg.org/veg/Orgs/VegSocUK/info.html
The Vendor Showcase	http://www.hospitalitynet.nl/v/alpha.htm
The Virtual Bar	http://www.TheVirtualBar.com
The Wine House	http://www.virtually.com/plaza/winehouse/champagne.html
The Wine Page	http://www.speakeasy.org/~winepage/wine.html
The World Cheese Index	http://www.wgx.com/cheesenet/wci/
The World Wide Web of Beer	http://www.nycbeer.org/links/
The YellowWeb Shopping Mall	http://www.yweb.com/shopping/mall09en.html
Todd & Holland Tea Merchants [tea1]	http://www.branchmall.com/teas/teas.html
U Brew Seattle	http://www.poppyware.com/ubrew/
Ultimate Beer Page	http://www.caiw.nl/~rbgoudsw/index.html
Universal Power Systems at	http://www.tecsolv.com/pizza/prices.htm
Uroulette	http://kuhttp.cc.ukans.edu/vwis/organizations/kucia/uroulette/uroulette.html
Vegetarian pasta salad	http://starburst.cbl.cees.edu/~tara/pastasalad.html
Vegetarian Pages	http://www.veg.org/veg/
Veggie Heaven	http://www.webserve.co.uk/Veggie/
Vietconnection cooking	http://vietconnection.com/Arts/Aitems.map?39,105
Vietnamese Cooking	http://vietconnection.com/Arts/cooking/recipes/Appetizer/Spring-Roll.htm
Vietnamese French and Chinese cooking	http://vietconnection.com/Arts/cooking/Cooking.htm
Vintage Direct	http://www.sofcom.com.au/Nicks/Cookbooks.html
Virtual Wine Country	http://www.wines.com/tasttop.html
Visit Upstate New York	http://www.spinners.com/tompcoliving/food2.html
Warehouse Coffeetopia	http://www.webventure.com/coffeetopia/index.cgi
Watermelon Gazpacho	http://foodstuff.com/pearl/rec-sou.html.
WebMenu	http://www.webmenu.com/
Wegman's Recipes	http://www.wegmans.com/kitchen/recipes/soups.html
Where beer is brewed	http://www.nycbeer.org/brewpubs.html
Where beer is tasted	http://www.nycbeer.org/drinking.html
Where beer is bought	http://www.nycbeer.org/stores.html
Why Coffee is Better Than Women	http://www.me.mtu.edu/~loew/coffee_women.html
Wine Country Inn	http://www.napavalley.com/napavalley/lodging/inns/wcinn/index.html
Wine Country Inn	http://www.napavalley.com/napavalley/outdoor/chargolf/chargolf.html
Wines on the Internet	http://www.wines.com/
World Beer Direct	http://www.worldbeerdirect.com/
X-Rated Chocolates	http://www.eden.com/~plainwrp/choco/
Xerox Map Viewer	http://pubweb.parc.xerox.com/map
Yahoo!	http://www.yahoo.com/
Yahoo!Beer	http://www.yahoo.com/Entertainment/Drinks_and_Drinking/Alcoholic_Drinks/Beer/Personal_Beer_Pages/
Yahoo! Cookbook	http://gnn.yahoo.com/gnn/Entertainment/Food_and_Eating/Recipes/Cookbooks
Yahoo! quick breads	http://home.sn.no/~gwalther/bajas.htm
Yale University's link to the Middle East	http://www.cs.yale.edu/homes/hupfer/global/regions/mideast.html#israel
Yan Can Cook (and so can kids)	http://www.2way.com.food/egg/egg0296/kidscook.html
Yiddish Recipe Archives	ftp://sunsite.unc.edu/pub/academic/languages/yiddish/recipes/
Zagat Dine homepage	http://pathfinder.com/Travel/Zagat/Dine/index.html.

ILLUSTRATION CREDITS

The following illustrations are reproduced with permission:

Pages 6, 157, from CondeNast.
Page 22, from Digital Equipment Corporation.
Pages 48, 49, from FoodNet.
Page 60, from HomeArts, Inc., copyright 1997, The Hearst
    Corporation.
Page 65, from Pumpkin Patch.
Page 66, from Caprialts Kitchen.
Page 71, from Virtual Bar.
Page 75, from the Italian Classic Cupboard.
Page 87, from Julie Rampke.
Page 89, from Thomas Lange.
Pages 99, 100, 101, from Kyle Whelliston.
Pages 110, 112, from Charles Hall.
Page 118, from Todd & Holland Tea Merchants, copyright 1996.
Pages 127, 128, from Jarrett Pashel.
Pages 129, 133, from Wines on the Internet.
Pages 137, 143, from the National Confectioners Association.
Page 140, from Maisha Marsh Birchall.
Pages 151, 152, from Butterball, Inc.
Page 153, from Pam Bumgardner.
Page 159, from Stylish Hats.
Page 176, from electronic Gourmet Guide.
Page 182, from Zagat.
Page 184, from Cuisine Net, Inc.
Page 185, from Richard Lagerling.
Page 192, from the Culinary Institute of America.
Page 197, from Margaret Cowan Direct, Ltd.
Page 201, from Pam Lester.
Pages 206, 208, from Barry Cinnamon.

INDEX